Aspects of Applied Geography

RIVER BASIN MANAGEMENT

Alan Doherty
(Principal Teacher of Geography, Linlithgow Academy)

Malcolm McDonald
(Principal Teacher of Geography, Bathgate Academy)

Series editor: Martin Duddin
(Assistant Rector, Knox Academy, Haddington)

Hodder & Stoughton

A MEMBER OF THE HODDER HEADLINE GROUP

ACKNOWLEDGEMENTS

CONTENTS

The author and publishers thank the following for permission to reproduce photographs and material in this book: Oxford Science Library (cover); Camera Press (1.1); United States Department of the Interior. Bureau of Reclamation (1.25, 1.26); Jim Bruce (2.8); Chris Riddell (2.16); Frank Dabba Smith (2.19); The Ecologist (3.5); The New Internationalist (3.7, 4.2); Mark Edwards (4.3); David Jones (4.4,4.8); Penguin (The Cadillac Desert, page 39).

Every effort has been made to contact the holders of copyright material but if any have been inadvertently overlooked, the publisher will be pleased to make the necessary alterations at the first opportunity.

British Library Cataloguing in Publication Data

Doherty, Alan
River Basin Management - (Aspects of applied geography Series)
I Title II McDonald, Malcolm III series
910.91

ISBN 0 340 55394 4
First published 1992
Impression number 13 12 11 10 9 8 7 6 5 4
Year   1999 1998 1997 1996 1995 1994
Copyright © 1992 Alan Doherty and Malcolm McDonald

Printed in Great Britain for Hodder & Stoughton Educational, a division of Hodder Headline Plc, 338 Euston Road, London NW1 3BH by Redwood Books, Trowbridge, Wiltshire.

The cover shows a Landsat image of Cairo and the Nile delta. The black thread of the river Nile can be seen surrounded by a thin strip of red vegetation which opens into the wide mouth of the delta. Cairo is visible as the light blue area at the head of the delta, just before the river forks into the Rosetta Nile (left) and the Damietta Nile (right). Light blue areas in the delta are other cities.

WATER

Our Planet's Most Valuable Resource

Freshwater is a limited resource. There is only so much of it circulating throughout the planet's ecosystems. An adequate and reliable supply of water for agriculture, industry and people can only be ensured by the active management of water resources.

WATER MEANS LIFE AND DEATH!

Precipitation makes the rivers flow, waters our farmlands, quenches the population's thirst, and provides an important means of transport and a cheap source of power. However, the same precipitation often falls as acid rain, dissolves fertilisers and pesticides, flushes effluents, carries water based diseases (schistosomiasis, cholera, typhoid, dysentery and diarrhoea) and intermittently floods river valleys causing death and destruction.

Water is a unique substance. The global water system or hydrological system has a marked effect on our planet's atmosphere. Water heats up and cools down more slowly than the Earth's land surfaces, thus producing a narrower temperature range than would exist on a waterless planet. The resulting equable

Figure1.1 Flooding in Bangladesh

environment is dominated by life forms which are composed mainly of water and whose existence depends totally on this most basic resource.

The Earth's water volume (km³)

River channels	1700
Swamps and marshes	3600
Moisture in soil	65 000
Water in plants	65 000
Saline lakes and inland seas	104 000
Atmospheric water	113 000
Freshwater lakes and reservoirs	125 000
Ice caps and glaciers	30 000 000
Groundwater	4 - 60 000 000
Oceans and open seas	1 370 000 000

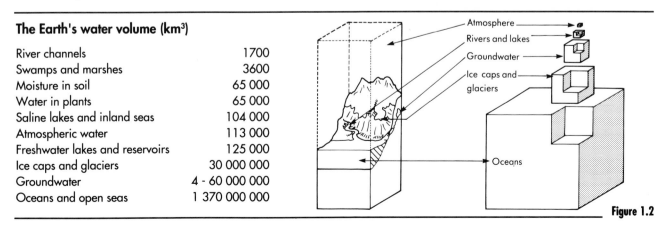

Figure 1.2

WATER AS A FINITE RESOURCE

There are approximately 1.4 billion cubic kilometres (km³) of water within our planet's hydrosphere. Nearly 3 per cent of this is freshwater (see figure1.2), 77.2 per cent of this freshwater is in 'cold storage' locked up in glaciers and ice caps and 22.4 per cent is groundwater and soil moisture. This leaves only a very small amount of surface freshwater – 0.35 per cent in lakes and swamps and less than 0.01 per cent in rivers and streams.

There is a huge amount of water in the hydrosphere but only a relatively small amount is available for human use and consumption (see figure 1.2). Moreover this limited resource is often in the wrong place at the wrong time or in the wrong quality to be used efficiently. It is therefore not surprising that people have sought from the earliest times to control and harness the rivers. Successful water engineering was the cornerstone of early civilisations, including the Persian, the Roman and the Egyptian. Control over river water nowadays is dominated in both the Developed and Developing World by the constructions of ever larger dams.

These dams are used to try to even out the distribution of water within the river basin. Figure 1.3 shows the different type of river regimes throughout the world. In simple terms it shows at which points in the year the rivers will be carrying the most water.These differences are caused by climatic features such as wet/dry seasons, temperature changes and snow melt.

The relative amount of water available for use in any given area is governed by the hydrological cycle and the population density; the larger the population, the more people there are competing for water resources. Ancient Egyptians, for example, had access to approximately the same amount of water as the modern Egyptians do. The critical difference is population. In 1000 BC there were less than 1 million Egyptians; today there are 47 million.

Not only are increasing populations leading to competing demands on the global water resource but freshwater is now used in an expanding variety of ways. Clearly societies must learn to use existing resources more efficiently. This is the key to successful river basin management.

1 Use an atlas to discover the temperature range experienced on Earth. If possible compare this range with that of the planet Mars.
2 What is meant by an equable environment?
3 Study figure 1.2. Calculate the total amount of freshwater in the hydrological cycle which is readily available for human use. Answer in cubic kilometres.
4 List some of the ways in which our range of uses for water has expanded.
5 Water is often in the wrong place at the wrong time, and of the wrong quality to be used efficiently. Discuss with reference to figure 1.1.
6 Pick out two areas in the world and describe how the river regime will cause problems for water users.
7 Which areas have the greatest imbalance between high and low levels of river flow?

Figure 1.3

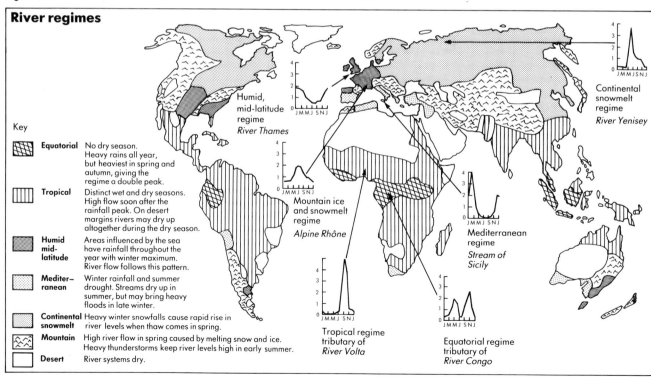

River regimes

Key

Equatorial	No dry season. Heavy rains all year, but heaviest in spring and autumn, giving the regime a double peak.
Tropical	Distinct wet and dry seasons. High flow soon after the rainfall peak. On desert margins rivers may dry up altogether during the dry season.
Humid mid-latitude	Areas influenced by the sea have rainfall throughout the year with winter maximum. River flow follows this pattern.
Mediter-ranean	Winter rainfall and summer drought. Streams dry up in summer, but may bring heavy floods in late winter.
Continental snowmelt	Heavy winter snowfalls cause rapid rise in river levels when thaw comes in spring.
Mountain	High river flow in spring caused by melting snow and ice. Heavy thunderstorms keep river levels high in early summer.
Desert	River systems dry.

Humid, mid-latitude regime
River Thames

Continental snowmelt regime
River Yenisey

Mountain ice and snowmelt regime
Alpine Rhône

Mediterranean regime
Stream of Sicily

Tropical regime tributary of *River Volta*

Equatorial regime tributary of *River Congo*

The Hydrological Cycle - macro scale

EVAPORATION is the process of water changing from a liquid into a gas. An input of energy (solar radiation) causes this change.

CONDENSATION is the process of water changing from a vapour to a liquid. Condensation takes place when water vapour is cooled.

PRECIPITATION
Rain, snow, hail and sleet are the main forms of precipitation. Precipitation is difficult to record accurately.

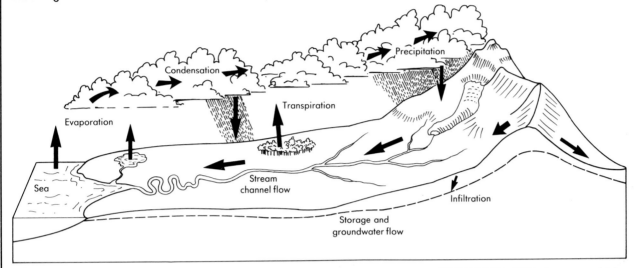

TRANSPIRATION is the process of water loss from plants. Transpiration takes place when the vapour pressure in the air is less than that in the leaf cells, ie transpiration is nil when the relative humidity of the air is 100 per cent. In the absence of plant cover, evaporation would still occur from the soil.

EVAPOTRANSPIRATION is the combination of evaporation and transpiration from an area. GROUNDWATER is derived mainly from precipitation which has percolated through the soil layers into the zone of saturation, where all pores and cracks are water-filled.

STREAM RUN OFF is the water which finds its way back to the sea via river channels. It is made up of two components; a highly variable storm run off, and a more predictable stable run off (base flow).

Figure 1.4

Approximately 453 000 cubic kilometres of water are evaporated from the surface of the world's oceans each year. Roughly 90 per cent of this water vapour returns to the oceans as precipitation, while the remaining 41 000km^3 is transported over the continents, where, after combining with over 72 000km^3 of evaporation and transpiration from the land masses, it condenses to fall as precipitation (see figure 1.4). It is this annual flow of 113 000km^3 which sustains the natural and human ecosystems on earth. A balance is maintained between the inflow of moisture to the continents and the outflow of water from the rivers and groundwater aquifers to the sea. (see table 1a). Water is unusual in that it can exist in all three matter states at a single location on the globe.

It is the amount of stable run off - the dependable flow of water in rivers - which determines how much water is actually available for human use on a year round basis. It excludes water which cannot be reliably tapped by humans, ie high seasonal flows

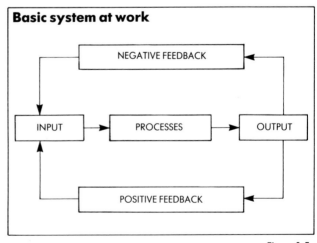

Figure 1.5

and floods. However if this water is stored in reservoirs it increases the dependable flow of water or stable run off available to the local population.

GLOBAL WATER SURPLUS AND DEFICIENCY

The hydrological cycle does not spread water evenly over the globe. Great differences in the availability of water exist over relatively small areas. On a macro or global scale there appears to be no scarcity of water. Over 41 000 cubic kilometres of water fall over the continents. The stable run off amounts to 13 000km³ annually, but as around 5000km³ flows through sparsely populated regions, the total volume of water readily available for human use is reduced to 8000km³ per year. Spread evenly such a volume would ensure that no areas of water shortage could exist, no matter how intensive the demand for water. The variability of the precipitation pattern however, is inevitably reflected in river flow, and the world can therefore be divided into areas of sufficiency and deficiency

Sufficiency may be measured in terms of vegetation water requirements (see figure 1.6) or in terms of stable run off per capita (see table 1a).

8 Examine figure 1.6. Describe the distribution of the world's main areas of water deficiency or chronic water shortage.
9 What are the advantages of identifying areas of water deficiency in terms of annual precipitation and evapotranspiration compared with the stable run off figures in table 1a.
10 Comment on the per capita water availability in the USA, Egypt, and China.
11 In what ways could the stable run off in an area be increased?

TOTAL AND PER CAPITA WATER SUPPLIES AVAILABLE IN CERTAIN COUNTRIES

Water rich countries	Total (km³ per year)	Per capita'000 cubic metres per year
Canada	3122	12193
Panama	144	6606
Nicaragua	175	5348
Brazil	5190	3828
Ecuador	314	3348
Malaysia	456	2932
Sweden	183	2211
Cameroon	208	2141
Finland	104	2133
Soviet Union	4174	1693
Indonesia	2530	1534
Austria	90	1202
USA	2478	1043
Water poor countries		
China	2680.000	252
India	185.000	243
Peru	40.000	203
Haiti	11.000	167
Poland	58.800	157
South Africa	50.000	154
Belgium	12.500	127
Egypt	56.000	120
Kenya	14.800	72
Oman	0.660	54
Barbados	0.053	20
Libya	0.700	19
Malta	0.025	7

Table 1a

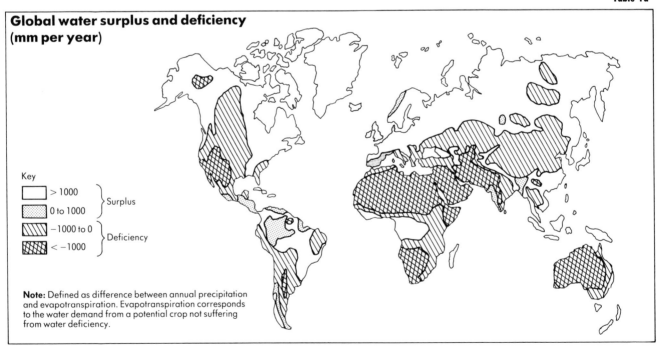

Global water surplus and deficiency (mm per year)

Key
- > 1000 } Surplus
- 0 to 1000 }
- −1000 to 0 } Deficiency
- < −1000 }

Note: Defined as difference between annual precipitation and evapotranspiration. Evapotranspiration corresponds to the water demand from a potential crop not suffering from water deficiency.

Figure 1.6

The Hydrological Cycle - micro scale

The journey of a molecule of water round the water cycle is not quite as simple as that shown in figure 1.4. It could leave the ocean by evaporation, join a cloud by condensation, and then fall back into the ocean ready to start again. One third of our planet, however, is land with a variety of slopes and vegetation cover. Water movement over and under the surface becomes part of a highly complex system known as a drainage basin. This is the area which collects the precipitation, which, if not used up or 'lost', ends up in a river channel. Looking at the drainage basin as a system allows the different factors to be studied individually and to see the knock on effects the change in one part will have on another. Only after this has been done, can the real complexity of water movement within the drainage basin be fully appreciated.

EVAPOTRANSPIRATION - OUTPUT

Evaporation operates on all surface areas such as the ground, vegetation, streams, rivers, lakes and reservoirs. Lake Mead, one of the largest reservoirs in the Colorado Basin, can lose annually the amount of water it would take to cover 1000 football pitches with one metre of water. In desert areas the potential evaporation is sometimes greater than the average rainfall over a particular period. If this happens then little, if any, of the precipitation can be guaranteed for agricultural or domestic use.

INFILTRATION OR RUN OFF

The speed and amount of rainwater which percolates down through the soil will depend on several factors. These are shown in table 1b. All of these factors affect the infiltration capacity of the surface. This is the total volume of water which can pass through the soil within a set period of time. As soon as this level is exceeded then there will be a surface run off of moisture.

A raindrop could
- evaporate
- run downhill (surface run off)
- be stored by plants (stemflow)
- sink into the ground (infiltration)
- end up in a river, lake or reservoir (storage).

SURFACE RUN OFF VARIABLES

Surface run off		Infiltration
Little or no vegetation	VEGETATION	Dense forest or cropland
Impermeable rock, eg granite	INFILTRATION	Very permeable rock, eg chalk
Very steep slope	ANGLE OF SLOPE	Gentle slope or flat land
Built up area of a city	LAND COVER	Farmland
Close to the surface	DEPTH OF WATER TABLE	Great distance from the surface
Storm or heavy intensive rain	INTENSITY OF PRECIPITATION	Very gentle but steady fall

Figure 1.7   Table 1b

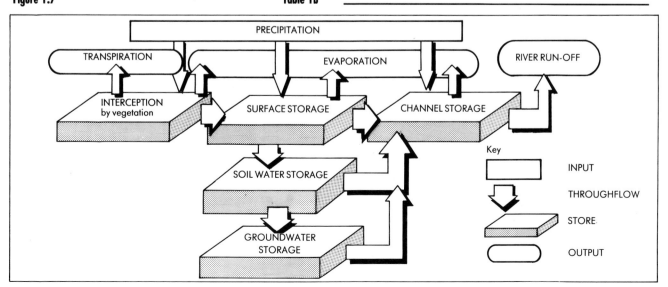

12 Describe the effect that precipitation falling as snow will have on the drainage basin system.
13 Describe and explain the differences in summer and winter in an area of deciduous woodland in Britain.
14 What effects will the construction of large reservoirs have on the system?
15 In an area of water shortage explain why some farmers are trying to make their fields more level by using terraces.
16 Why will a farmer favour a soil which has a good balance between infiltration and its storage capacity?

VEGETATION COVER - STORE

The greater the amount of vegetation, the less water will actually reach the ground. The moisture will eventually work its way down to the ground via the stem or by dripping from the leaves. If there is a large mass of vegetation, as exists in a deciduous forest, then the roots will absorb some of this moisture, and it will be retained or stored within the plants themselves. Prior to deforestation the forest cover acts as a check on precipitation by holding back water from surface run off and river channels. Much of the flooding, for example, in the lower part of the Ganges and Brahmaputra has been attributed to the clearing of the forests of the lower slopes of the Himalayas. The erosive strength of the rainwater is no longer held back by the thick foliage and the soil is easily eroded and transported. This process has added a vast amount of sediment to the river's load which in turn has raised the level of the river in periods of exceptional rainfall. This has contributed to the disastrous flooding which has been so evident in recent years.

PERMEABILITY

One of the most important factors in determining the level of run off (see table 1b) is the surface permeability. If a rock allows water to pass down through it, then it is **permeable**. Permeability has two forms. If the rock has lots of spaces between the different grains then it is very porous. Sandstone has a porosity of between 20 per cent and 25 per cent. The pore spaces are the gaps between the individual grains of sand when they were initially deposited. Some rocks, like granite, are more crystalline and there are very few gaps which can be filled by water (one per cent).

If a rock is **pervious**, it has numerous faults or joints running through it allowing water to move downwards quite easily. In some cases the water will be able to widen these joints by dissolving away material and the enlarged gaps will let even more water pass through at a quicker rate. The best example of this type of chemical weathering is found in limestone.

SUB SURFACE ZONES - STORE

Some of the water which percolates down into the soil surface remains in the **zone of aeration** and the **capillary fringe**. See figure 1.8. The zone of aeration is the surface layer of soil where the pore spaces are not filled with water. This is the most important zone for plant growth and the air spaces and a film of moisture sticking to the soil particles allow plants to flourish. The capillary fringe is the soil zone immediately above the water table. Water is drawn up into this area by capillary action. This capillary movement in soils is very important when looking at water management problems in areas of high irrigation because the vertical movement of water up through the soil tends to bring with it soluble salts which can have a very damaging effect on the overall quality of the soil for agricultural and domestic purposes.

Figure 1.8

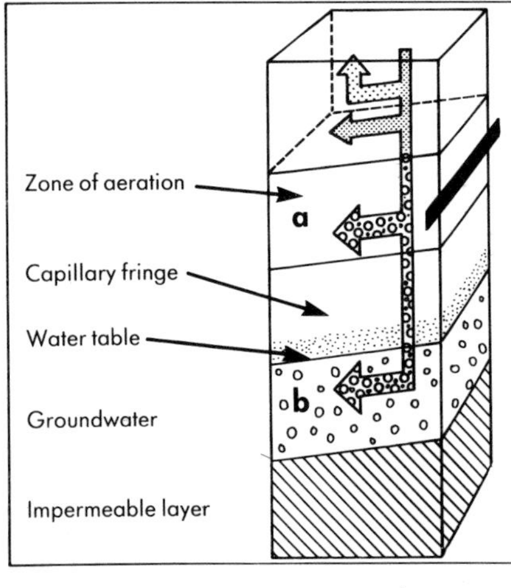

Key
a Sub surface water movement occurs when the soil is saturated and the excess water flows down hill as sub surface throughflow.
b Groundwater will move horizontally along rock strata. This movement is called baseflow and usually occurs when river levels drop and the lost water is replaced by incoming base flow. This is the reason why rivers will still have some flow even after long periods without precipitation.

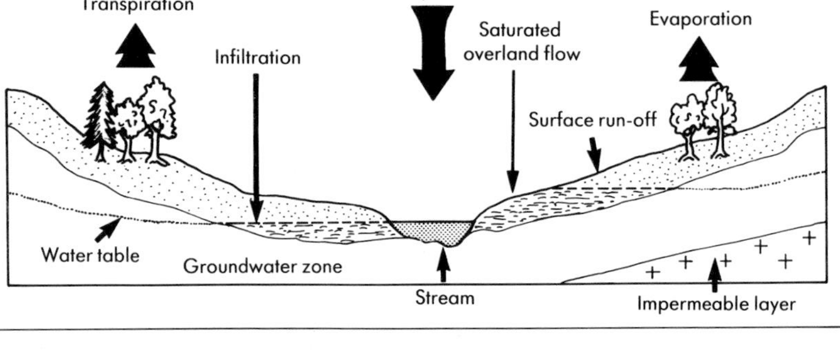

GROUNDWATER - STORE

Water will percolate down through the soil until it reaches an impermeable layer. The water will fill up the spaces above this impermeable zone forming the zone of saturation. This **groundwater** can be stored or transferred downslope depending on the layout of the rocks underground. The **water table** is the uppermost level of this saturated zone or aquifer. In areas where surface water is scarce, this underground reservoir forms an important addition to the water supplies. In some areas, like the Lower Colorado it is being 'mined' faster than it can be replaced, with the result that the water table has fallen by more than 10 metres per year in one area of Arizona. This has led to ground level subsidence and a decrease in water quality, as the pumps now bring water up from rocks with deposits of salt and gypsum.

17 In a landscape untouched by human interference describe the areas where water is stored both above and below the surface.

18 Why are geologists, looking for underground supplies of water, more likely to be interested in sandstone rather than igneous rocks?

19 Make your own copy of figure 1.8 and use the text to help you add your own definitions of all the terms.

Hydrographs

WATER MEASUREMENT

Before encouraging human use of water within a river basin it would obviously be sensible to gauge the amount of water available and the changes in availability throughout the year. In the ideal world, proper planning for water use would need data on several variables, such as annual precipitation, intensity of rainfall, potential evaporation, soil infiltration capacity and volume of water in the groundwater store. Because of the expense of collecting such a mass of data, the water engineer usually has to make plans based only on annual precipitation and the **discharge** of the river. The discharge is the amount of water passing a particular sampling point on the river. By measuring the channel shape and the speed of the river, the volume of water is calculated. In areas where the height of the river varies throughout the year it is important to know: i) the expected base flow
ii) the maximum height of peak flows during periods of strong storms or excessive snow melt in the catchment area.

This can be analysed in a storm hydrograph (see figure 1.9). These are of great value when looking at the storage capacities of reservoirs, the prediction of floods and the stabilising of river flow throughout the year.

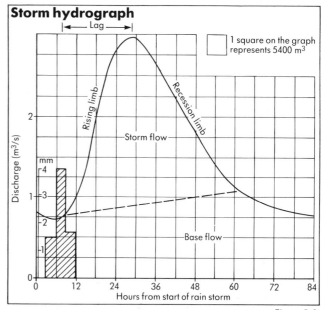

Figure 1.9

INTERPRETATION

The hydrograph gives information on the volume of storm water entering the river as discharge and its lag time. The more intense the precipitation, the less chance the moisture has of percolating down through the soil and therefore the greater the amount of surface run off. Various physical processes shape the river channel through time and enable it to carry a certain amount of water. When the volume builds up faster than the river can carry the water away, the height of the river increases rapidly until it reaches what is known as bankfull discharge. Once this level has been reached any increase will result in an overland flow or flood.

Study figure 1.9
20 How many hours did the storm last?
21 At what time was the peak discharge?
22 How much water was passing the gauging station at the height of the storm?
23 What was the total volume of water produced by the storm in excess of the base flow?
24 Describe and explain what effect there will be on the rising limb, peak discharge and falling limb under the following conditions:
a) Intense storm in an area suffering from a two month drought.
b) Long period of steady rain in an area of dense woodland in the middle of summer.
c) Storm in an area of chalk soils covered in grass.

RISING LIMB

The first excess flow to pass the gauging station is the rainwater which fell into the streams themselves. The rain falling over the catchment area takes longer to reach the station as some of it will have percolated down into the top layers of the soil. As the saturation of the soil increases, an increasing amount of water will be forced to run across the surface as overland flow and into the stream channels. This leads to a peak discharge.

The shape of the limb will depend on the length and intensity of the rainstorm and the condition of the soil itself. If the soil is already saturated more water will get into the streams and lead to a higher and earlier peak discharge.

LAG TIME

The lag time shown in figure 1.9 is the difference between the time the rain actually fell and the time the bulk of it passed the gauging station. This point is called the peak discharge. This lag time will be longer if the soil is drier, the slopes more gentle, or the rain falls at a prolonged but steady pace. The length of the lag time will obviously vary with the size of the drainage basin and the position of the gauging station.

FALLING LIMB

This section of the hydrograph shows the speed at which the drainage of the river basin returns to normal (base flow) once the storm has passed and the rain stopped.

Look at figure 1.10 and answer the following questions:

25 Match the gauging stations (1-5) with the descriptions of the river basins (A-E) and the storm hydrographs (V-Z). Explain your choices.
26 What difference will there be in the lag time for a river basin with an impermeable rock compared with a permeable rock?
27 Draw the hydrographs for area 5 assuming the whole of the catchment area is covered by a full grown coniferous plantation.
28 Draw out the possible hydrographs for the four river basin shapes below. Vegetation, rock type and precipitation are the same for each.

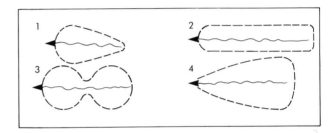

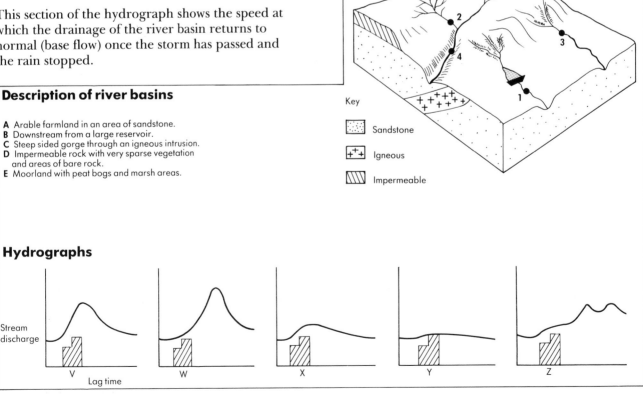

Description of river basins

A Arable farmland in an area of sandstone.
B Downstream from a large reservoir.
C Steep sided gorge through an igneous intrusion.
D Impermeable rock with very sparse vegetation and areas of bare rock.
E Moorland with peat bogs and marsh areas.

Key

░░ Sandstone

+++ Igneous

▨ Impermeable

Hydrographs

Stream discharge

V   W   X   Y   Z

Lag time

Figure 1.10

Drainage Basin Characteristics

Drainage basins make excellent subjects for investigations. There are several features which can be easily measured and then used to make comparisons between basins, or to work out the effect of geology, climate, vegetation, or slope on the patterns of a drainage basin. Using large scale maps and fieldwork it is possible to record a series of statistics about any river basin.

Some of the measurements which help to define the form of drainage basins are:

- Stream orders
- Bifurcation ratios
- Drainage density
- Stream order correlations
- Basin order correlations
- Channel patterns
- Drainage patterns.

STREAM ORDERING

When looking at the shape of a stream network one of the most important features is the stream order of the river basin. This is a system devised by an American geographer called Strahler. All the 'finger-tip' tributaries are called first order streams. When two first order streams meet they form a second order stream. An example is shown below.

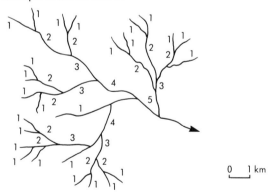

After the network has been drawn out and then ordered it is possible to look at the stream orders and compare them with other sets of measurements which can be done on the river basin. These might include:
- Average length of the streams in each order
- Links between the number of streams in each order
- Links between the gradients of the streams in each order
- Relationship between the average basin size of the streams in each stream order.

Figure 1.11

BIFURCATION RATIO

This can be simply defined as the ratio between the number of streams in one order to the number of streams in the next order. The bifurcation ratio is usually between 3.0 and 5.0 in basins where the geology is not a dominant influence on the drainage pattern.

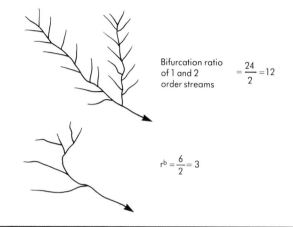

Bifurcation ratio of 1 and 2 order streams $= \dfrac{24}{2} = 12$

$r^b = \dfrac{6}{2} = 3$

Figure 1.12

DRAINAGE DENSITIES

The lengths of the streams are measured (km) and compared with the area in square kilometres.

Drainage density $= \dfrac{\text{Sum of all stream lengths}}{\text{Total area of the basin}}$

The answer or value which is worked out indicates how frequently streams occur on the map area. Drainage densities are higher where there are impermeable rocks, high precipitation and steep slopes. The density of vegetation also affects the value as it binds the surface together and limits the amount of surface flow which might lead to the erosion of soil and the formation of small stream channels.

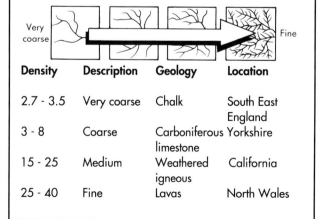

Density	Description	Geology	Location
2.7 - 3.5	Very coarse	Chalk	South East England
3 - 8	Coarse	Carboniferous limestone	Yorkshire
15 - 25	Medium	Weathered igneous	California
25 - 40	Fine	Lavas	North Wales

Figure 1.13

STREAM ORDER CORRELATION

You would expect the lower order streams to be smaller in length than the higher order streams. If you want to test this hypothesis you could measure all the streams of each order, work out the average for each order then plot the results on graph paper to see if there is any relationship.

If one set of figures increases or decreases directly with an increase in another set of figures it is possible to work out the statistical relationship or correlation between the two. Two examples are shown below:

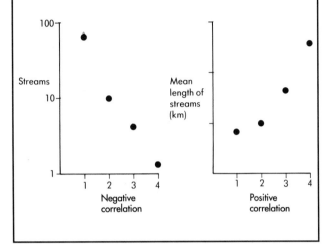

Figure 1.14

BASIN AREA CORRELATION

The area of the drainage basin is measured and then plotted to see what relationship, if any, exists between the different stream orders.

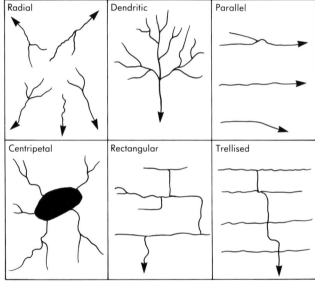

Figure 1.15

CHANNEL DESCRIPTIONS

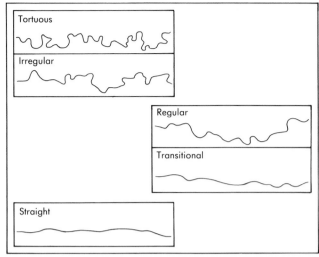

Figure 1.16

DRAINAGE PATTERNS

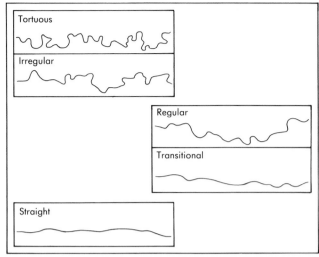

Figure 1.17

29 Calculate the bifurcation ratio of first and second order streams in the drainage basin in figure 1.11.

30 Complete a copy of the table (figure 1.18) and measure the length of the streams of each order in figure 1.11. Calculate the mean length, as in figure 1.14, to see if there is any correlation between the average length of stream and the stream order.

31 Is there any correlation between the number of streams in each order and the stream order for the drainage basin in figure 1.11?
Use log paper to plot the figures for each stream order and draw a best fit line. Refer to figure 1.14.

32 Make a tracing of the drainage basin in figure 1.11. Place this tracing over a piece of centimetre graph paper. Calculate the area in square kilometres. If you refer to figure 1.13 you should now be able to work out the drainage density for this river basin.

NOTES		Second order streams	
First order streams		1	7
1	10	19	2	8
2	11	20	3	9
3	12	21	4	10
4	13	22	5	11
5	14	23	6	
6	15	24		
7	16	25	Total length of second	
8	17	26	order streams =	
9	18		Average length =	
Total length of				
first order streams =				
Average length =				

Figure 1.18

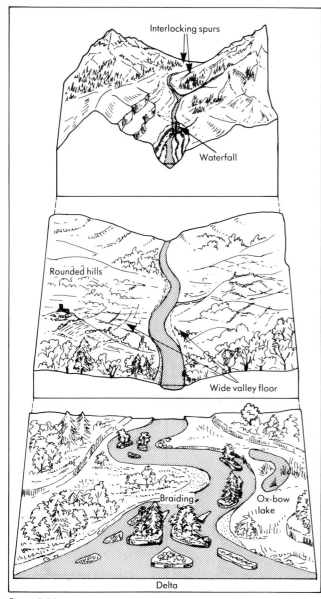

Figure 1.19

River Basin Landforms

The movement of water along a river channel is a very complex subject and the various processes involved lead to a great variety of physical landforms which can be seen in river basins of all scales throughout the world.

River courses may be conveniently divided into three main parts - the upper, middle and lower sections.

UPPER COURSE

In the upper course, the narrow v-shaped valleys are characterised by the presence of interlocking spurs, rapids, potholes (figure 1.20) and small waterfalls. On soft, easily eroded surface deposits the water may erode very small channels called rills which may then enlarge to form deep, v-shaped gullies. Cultivation in the upper course of a river increases soil erosion considerably.

MIDDLE COURSE

In its middle course, the river channel is much wider and the river flows between rounded hills. The river begins to meander in the more gentle gradient sections. In a meandering stream the water flows in a corkscrew path as the water tends to be flung to the outside of the bends and to compensate for this a return flow develops over the stream bed towards the inside of the bends (figure 1.22). The river profile in the middle course often consists of a series of steps as hard rock bands may inhibit the river's efforts to form a smoothly curving graded profile.

LOWER COURSE

In the lower course the river channel reaches its maximum width and maximum sinuosity (the number and width of bends) Meanders migrate a few metres downstream every year by continuous erosion from the outside of the bends and deposition on the inside bends (figure 1.21). In this way the floodplain alluvium is transported downstream (figure 1.21B). The lower course is characterised by floodplains, ox-bow lakes, meander scrolls and levees. Floodplain sediments may be cut through by the river and may form steps or platforms on the valley sides called terraces (figure 1.21A).

EROSION

Erosion by rivers takes place in three ways. Water can wear away the banks and bed of the river (hydraulic action). This process is more effective if the river is carrying a load to use as ammunition (corrasion). Rivers also erode by dissolving the rocks over which they flow (corrosion).

Potholes

Small pebbles are deposited in small hollows on the river bottom. The movement of the water rotates these stones and they 'drill' down into the river bed. The hole created catches other pebbles on their way downstream and they in turn help to increase the size of the potholes.

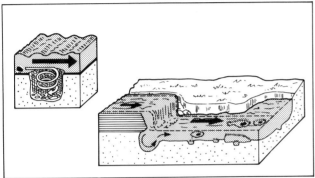

Figure 1.20

DISCHARGE

The discharge of the river is an important factor in shaping landforms along a river valley. The discharge of a river is the amount of water carried. It is measured in cubic metres per second, and is found by multiplying the average velocity by the cross-sectional area of the river. The width, depth, and velocity of a river increase as its discharge increases. Discharge increases downstream as channel width and depth increases.

PROCESSES

The shape or morphology of the valley floor and channel sides are the result of **erosion, transportation**, and **deposition**. All three processes may take place simultaneously along the entire length of a river. The discharge and nature of the material being carried (its load) control which process is dominant in any given area.

Figure 1.21

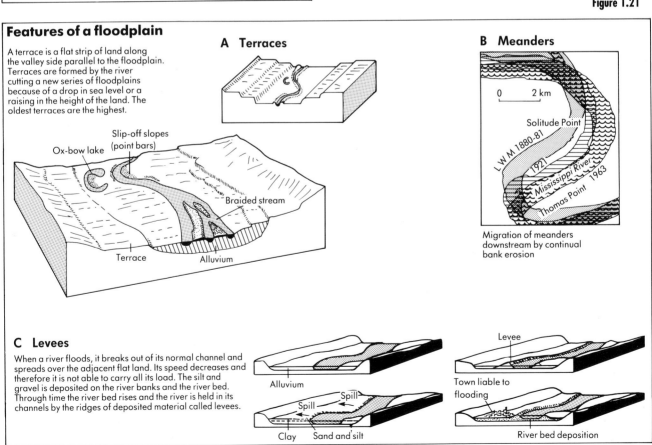

Features of a floodplain

A terrace is a flat strip of land along the valley side parallel to the floodplain. Terraces are formed by the river cutting a new series of floodplains because of a drop in sea level or a raising in the height of the land. The oldest terraces are the highest.

A Terraces

B Meanders

0   2 km

Solitude Point

L W M 1880-81
1921
Mississippi River
Thomas Point 1963

Migration of meanders downstream by continual bank erosion

Ox-bow lake
Slip-off slopes (point bars)
Braided stream
Terrace
Alluvium

C Levees

When a river floods, it breaks out of its normal channel and spreads over the adjacent flat land. Its speed decreases and therefore it is not able to carry all its load. The silt and gravel is deposited on the river banks and the river bed. Through time the river bed rises and the river is held in its channels by the ridges of deposited material called levees.

Alluvium
Spill
Spill
Clay   Sand and silt

Levee
Town liable to flooding
River bed deposition

Waterfalls

Waterfalls occur in the upper section where the river passes over a very resistant rock band or like the case in figure 1.20 a hard rock overlies a softer rock. The erosive power of the water wears away a plunge pool and the circular motion of the water eats away the softer rock and eventually leaves a large block of hard rock with no support. When it collapses into the river the waterfall has 'receded' upstream and the whole process starts again.

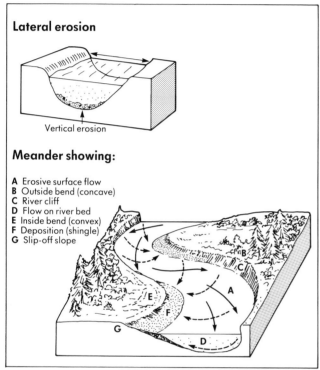

Lateral erosion

Vertical erosion

Meander showing:

A Erosive surface flow
B Outside bend (concave)
C River cliff
D Flow on river bed
E Inside bend (convex)
F Deposition (shingle)
G Slip-off slope

Figure 1.22

TRANSPORTATION

The suspended load consists of very small particles which are carried along in suspension without touching the bed of the stream. The bed load on the other hand, is moved by saltation, bouncing, rolling and sliding along the stream bed. In general the bed load is about one-tenth the mass of the suspended load.

DEPOSITION

Some shallow upland streams receive more sediment than they can transport. In this case the channel fills up with sediment and the river divides and rejoins around bars of sand and gravel. In such a braided stream (figure 1.21) the bed load may be more than a half of the total load. Deposition of transported material such as alluvium or sand takes place where turbulence and velocity decrease. Deposition may

take place where a stream runs suddenly from a steep mountain valley on to a plain or flat floored valley. The loss of energy leads the river to dump its load in the form of an alluvial fan.

Deposition also takes place on the inside of river bends because the velocity of the river is invariably slower there than on the outside of the bend. Such deposits are called point bars or slip-off slopes. In its lower course a river may deposit alluvium in the form of a flat floodplain. Where a river flows into a lake or into the sea it may deposit sediment in the form of a delta.

River Basin Management

'...Water is among the most essential requisites that nature provides to sustain life for plants, animals, and humans. The total quantity of fresh water on earth could satisfy all the needs of the human population if it were evenly distributed and accessible...'
W. Stumm, 1986

This basic problem has stimulated human development of river basins for the past 10 000 years. Early water management schemes were small scale and opportunistic, but through time, both the rate of dam or canal construction and the complexity of the resultant systems have increased. However, the last 30 years have seen an extraordinary growth in dam construction, stimulated by the need for protection against drought and the need to increase agricultural production and provide power for industrial development.

The modern history of river basin management can be traced back to two events in the 1930s. The first was the creation of the Tennessee Valley Authority (TVA) in the United States in 1934. The second was the Presidential address given to India's National Institute of Sciences in 1938 by Meghnad Salia, which helped set in motion the creation of the Damodar Valley Corporation (DVC) in 1948. Further river basin management schemes in India followed in quick succession but elsewhere in the Developing World the adoption of the river basin planning approach has not been taken up, with most countries concentrating on single large scale, high prestige projects. The decisions have been taken by engineers and bureaucrats with very little attention, if any, being given to the needs of the riverside population and the possible disturbance of the ecological balance. The resulting benefits have often been outweighed in many peoples' eyes by consequential adverse effects, and the 1980s and '90s have witnessed a backlash of environmental concern against large multi-purpose schemes. This concern has led to the adoption and promotion of an ecosystem approach to river basin management. Ultimately this would involve each project having to undergo a full environmental and social appraisal before construction was started.

It would look at:

- possible environmental effect on the drainage basin
- the effect on local people
- the full economic cost of improved agriculture
- possible effects on public health
- possible alternative power production
- long term feasibility taking into account silting up of the reservoirs.

This approach is considered further in chapter 3, although to date there are few examples of the ecological approach being adopted wholeheartedly in river basin management schemes.

MULTI-PURPOSE RIVER BASIN MANAGEMENT

Multi-purpose schemes have been seen as answers to basic water problems such as:

1 **Water supply**, or the provision of water for drinking, domestic use and irrigation. The basis of the water crisis in the eighties and nineties has been the continuing decline in the stable run off due to increases in population and per capita use. As the cartoon on page 28 shows, water quantity may be of more importance than water quality. All water management schemes should aim to provide water appropriate to the needs of the population being served.

2 **Flood control** Flooding is the most significant of all natural hazards accounting for nearly 2 per cent of all deaths globally each year. Flood damage is increasing despite the massive investment in flood control schemes. Many of the sites subject to flooding are also preferred locations for industry, commerce, and private housing.

The engineering response to flooding consists of using upstream storage or building levees and bypass channels to speed up water flow.

The ecological response to flooding aims to establish a natural plant cover, in the catchment area which would minimise the flow of water from the land phase.

3 **Hydro-electric power** is often a valuable by-product of integrated schemes. HEP production is often incompatible with flood control aims as the reservoirs are kept bankfull.

4 **Navigation** For a river to be navigable the water depth has to be kept above a certain level. Economically this is difficult to justify and in periods of low rainfall it is more important to store water for other uses.

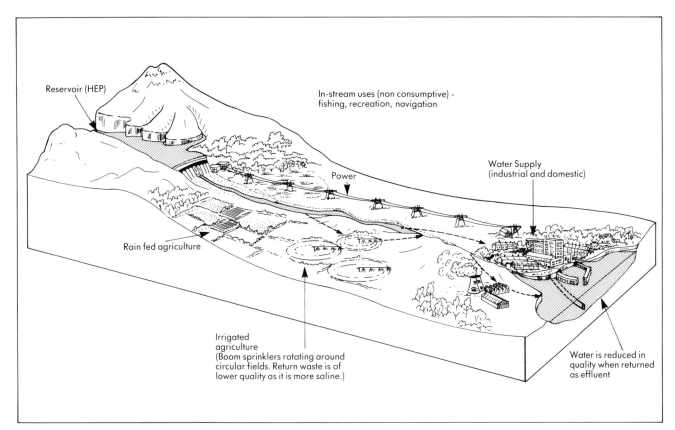

Reservoir (HEP)

In-stream uses (non consumptive) - fishing, recreation, navigation

Power

Water Supply (industrial and domestic)

Rain fed agriculture

Irrigated agriculture (Boom sprinklers rotating around circular fields. Return waste is of lower quality as it is more saline.)

Water is reduced in quality when returned as effluent

Figure 1.23

REGULATED RIVERS - MANAGEMENT METHODS

Small scale

For thousands of years people have tried to use rivers to their advantage. Early irrigators used small channels to carry water from the rivers to their field. Civilizations in the Midddle East , Central and South America and the south west of the present USA depended on irrigation for their survival. In the industrial era, rivers have been used as a source of power. To ensure that there was a large enough head of water to keep the water mill turning even when there was slightly less water in the river, weirs were built to raise the height.

Large scale

As technology has advanced the scope and size of river management schemes have increased. Schemes have been devised to make rivers run backwards and make water climb over or through mountains. Thousands of hectares of new farmland have been created and the power for many cities and industries comes directly from various river management schemes. The scale of dam constuction over the last 50 years can be seen in figure 1.24.

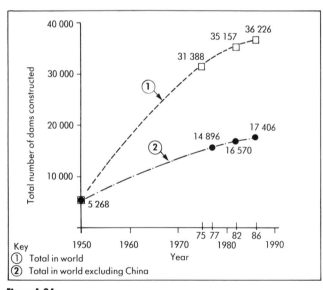

Figure 1.24

The Colorado

The Colorado, which will be studied in depth in the next chapter, in many ways exemplifies this human urge to control and subdue the natural environment. The USA, the richest country in the world, has devoted vast sums of money in building some of the largest dams and reservoirs in the world, irrigating deserts and sustaining huge desert cities and in harnessing the power of the river itself.

Figure 1.25 The Hoover Dam with Lake Mead behind it is just one of over 30 dams built along the Colorado and its tributaries.

Figure 1.26 Lake Mead water is treated in the huge Merrit Smith plant before it is sent onwards to southern Nevada. Water is diverted away from the river and is carried by a series of large canals.

SUMMARY

- The hydrological cycle is a good example of a natural system at work. Materials and energy move in a circular route. Inputs, stores, and outputs may be identified (figure 1.5), as the materials and energy are used and changed by processes at work in the system.
- Given the variable nature of the major components of the hydrological cycle - evaporation, precipitation, evapotranspiration, stream run off, and the contribution of groundwater - the world can therefore be divided into areas of sufficiency and deficiency.
- Subsurface water movement occurs when the soil is saturated and the excess water flows downhill as subsurface throughflow.
- Groundwater will move horizontally along rock strata. This movement is called baseflow and usually occurs when the river level drops and the lost water is replaced by incoming baseflow. This is the reason why rivers will still have some flow, even after long periods without precipitation.

2 THE COLORADO RIVER

KEY CONCEPTS

Location, Spacial pattern, Interdependence, Diversity, Change

'...Ours has been the first, and will doubtless be the last party to visit this profitless locality. It seems intended by nature that the Colorado along the greater part of its lonely and majestic way, shall be forever unvisited and undisturbed...'
Lt Joseph C Ives 1857 (explorer).

THE ENVIRONMENT

The Colorado Basin, at first sight, does seem an extremely inhospitable environment. Looking at the diagrams opposite the main problems facing the area can be easily diagnosed. It is extremely dry, with many areas receiving less than 25mm of annual precipitation. This is partly attributable to the rain shadow effect of the Sierra Nevada mountain range to the west of the river basin. Even this limited rainfall cannot be used because 95 per cent is lost through evaporation in an area with low humidity and daytime temperatures over 40°C. Summer heat and the winter cold expand and weaken rock fissures and keep the desert surfaces friable. The soils, with little vegetation to bind them, are very susceptible to erosion.

The rainfall is also very seasonal and in some summers there can be very violent thunderstorms bringing large volumes of water, but even that is lost through catastrophic flash floods and infiltration into the soil.

These conditions, along with the gradual elevation of the plateau, have caused unprecedented erosion in geologically recent times. The Colorado might not be the longest or biggest river in the world but in former times it was one of the most powerful and its name comes from the Spanish for 'ruddy' because of the huge amounts of sediment it was able to carry downstream. The Colorado, running through this parched landscape, is actually fed by the snow melt from the southern Rocky Mountains and the Wind River Range in Wyoming where the main tributary of the Colorado, the Green River, has its source. This leads to a great unpredictability in the amount and strength of the river flow. The annual variation and the long term variations can be seen in figure 2.4.

The historical annual flows, based on a study of tree rings within the upper basin of the Colorado, show persistent wet and dry cycles, measurable in decades. As we shall see later, this factor was not really taken into account when the waters of the Colorado were divided up in the 'Colorado River Compact' in 1922. It is only now that the people of the south west are beginning to realise the effect this mistake is going to have on the amount of water available and how it is going to be shared out.

1 **Describe the climatic features of the Colorado Basin which make water storage imperative.**
2 **Why is the annual flow so unpredictable?**
3 **What does the term 'rainfall variability' mean?**
4 **Why would 1917 and 1977 be bad years to choose for planners to base water allocation figures over a long period of time?**
5 **What physical and climatic features made the Colorado basin such an 'inhospitable environment'?**

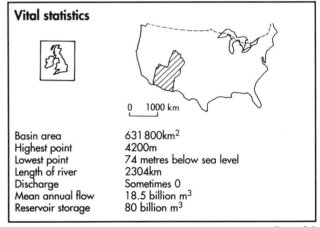

Vital statistics

Basin area	631 800km²
Highest point	4200m
Lowest point	74 metres below sea level
Length of river	2304km
Discharge	Sometimes 0
Mean annual flow	18.5 billion m³
Reservoir storage	80 billion m³

Figure 2.1

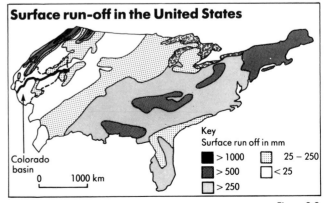

Surface run-off in the United States

Colorado basin

0   1000 km

Key
Surface run off in mm

■ > 1000
▨ > 500
▧ > 250
▦ 25 – 250
□ < 25

Figure 2.2

18

July temperatures in the United States

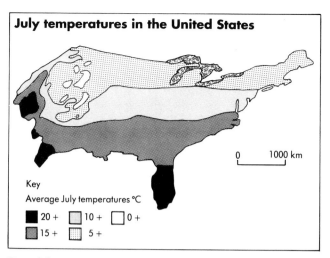

Key
Average July temperatures °C

- 20 +
- 15 +
- 10 +
- 5 +
- 0 +

0 — 1000 km

Figure 2.3

Annual discharge of the Colorado

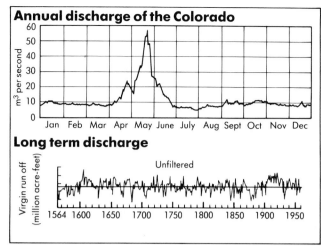

Long term discharge

Unfiltered

Figure 2.4

Colorado River Basin

States drained
Wyoming
Colorado
Utah
Nevada
Arizona
New Mexico
California

Discharge - per second
Colorado 503m³
Green   180m³
San Juan   74m³
Gunnison   73m³

Major rivers
UPPER COLORADO
1 Colorado
2 Green
3 Yampa
4 White
5 Gunnison
6 Dolores
7 San Juan

LOWER COLORADO
8 Virgin
9 Little Colorado
10 Bill Williams
11 Salt
12 Gila

Annual flow variation
1917 - 4.9km³
1977 - 21.4km³

A: Arizona
Ca: California
Co: Colorado
N: Nevada
NM: New Mexico
U: Utah
W: Wyoming

Depth - Colorado
Upper 3 metres
Lower 10 metres

Width - Colorado
First 80km = 15 metres
Grand Junction = 60 metres

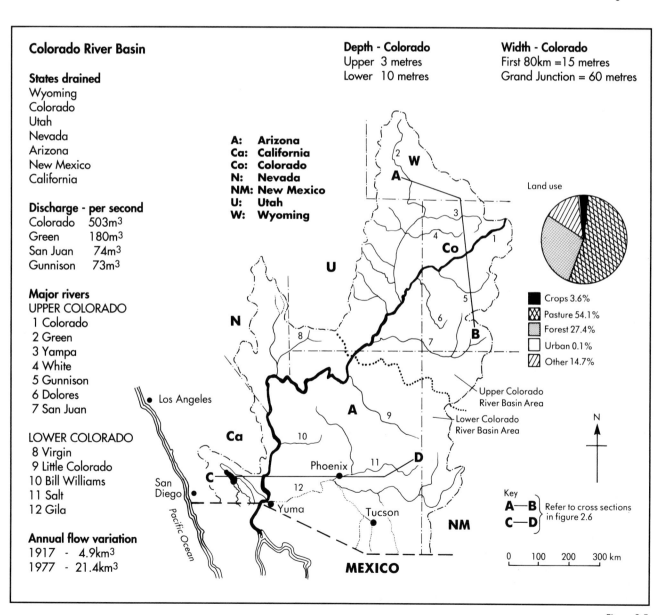

Land use

- Crops 3.6%
- Pasture 54.1%
- Forest 27.4%
- Urban 0.1%
- Other 14.7%

Upper Colorado
River Basin Area
Lower Colorado
River Basin Area

Key
A—B ⎫ Refer to cross sections
C—D ⎭ in figure 2.6

0   100   200   300 km

N

Figure 2.5

19

Upper Colorado

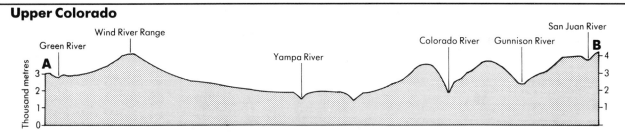

The Upper Colorado River Basin Area is bounded on the west, north and east by the Wasatch, Wind River and Sawatch Ranges, all of which make up, part of the Rocky Mountains. Some of these rugged mountains have peaks over 4200 metres. There are broad basins and high plateaus which contain deeply entrenched canyons carved by the Colorado and its tributaries. Most of the area has an arid to semi-arid climate and some areas receive less than 125mm of rainfall per annum while the highest peaks have subhumid to Alpine climates and often receive more than 1000mm. The variability of this rainfall is a real problem with figures ranging from 20 per cent to 200 per cent of the 'average'. Approximately 60 per cent of the land is owned by federal agencies or forms part of Indian lands.

Lower Colorado

The Lower Colorado River Basin Area makes up 5 per cent of the US land area. It is made up of a series of mountains, plains, deserts, and plateaus which range in height from 3851m down to 30m at Yuma. The basin and range area to the south west is made up of mountain chains and valleys separated by deeply dissected gorges. The plateau province is characterised by cliffs and slopes. These canyon lands are extensive next to the river, while low mesa-like features predominate in the south.

Figure 2.6

A Difficult Landscape?

The Colorado has carved a series of canyons into a great depth of horizontally laid out sedimentary rocks. Most of the various rocks, siltstones, sandstones, limestones and shales were formed in a variety of landscapes ranging from humid forested swamp land, vast sandy deserts, and shallow tropical seas. These canyons (see figure 2.7) were formed during a prolonged uplift of the whole area. It is not known why this occurred but the results have been quite spectacular. The river has cut like a cheese wire through the slowly rising rock and a combination of Bryce, Zion and the Grand Canyon, have exposed a total of 4500 metres of rock dating back to ancient schists of the basement rock estimated to be 1700 million years old.

The geological record is not quite complete and there are gaps or 'unconformities' where a rock of a certain age can be found lying on top of a rock which is much older. These occur at several points in the sequence and geologists believe that these rocks have been eroded en masse leaving no trace of their existence.

Grand Canyon

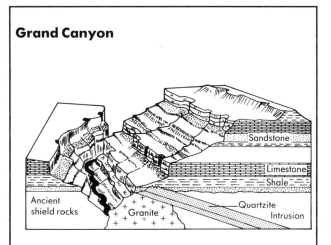

The whole slope of the Grand Canyon is controlled by the strength of the rock. The vertical cliffs are formed from the resistant sandstones and limestones. The weak shales form a gentle slope controlled by the angle of rest of the debris from the weathered shale.

Figure 2.7

6 Explain why the canyons of the Colorado are so suitable for the construction of large dams.
7 What problems would the engineers have faced when they found that the rocks on the sides of the canyons were of differing strengths?
8 What effect will the lack of vegetation and the amount of erosion have on the reservoirs?
9 Why will the creation of large reservoirs inevitably lead to the loss of more water?
10 Draw a cross-section of the Grand Canyon and add labels to show rock types, scree slopes, free faces, resistant granite and weak shale.

Figure 2.8 The Grand Canyon

Typical landscapes

Deeply **dissected plateau** with very deep **canyons** (the Grand Canyon is 1.9km deep). The lack of vegetation encourages heavy erosion leading to stable angle scree slopes. Most erosion takes place mechanically through wind abrasion or the effect of heat.

Eroded material is deposited by the streams to form huge **alluvial fans** which eventually join together along the base of the plateau.

Small **playa** (transitory lake) which may have a covering of clay or a crust of salt. Very flat salt lakes have been used for land speed attempts and spaceship landings. Examples in this area are Salt Lake and Lake Bonneville (Utah).

Wadis are steep sided valleys carved out by flash floods after the summer thunderstorms. They are deepened and widened by the great erosive strength of the floods. During the rest of the year they are dry but act as sources of groundwater.

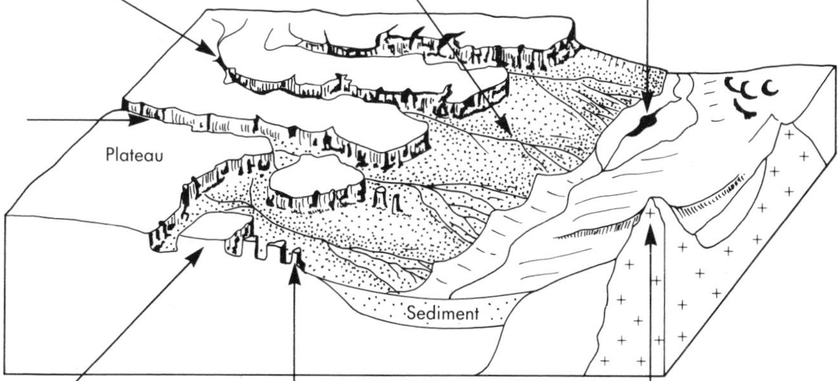

Plateau

Sediment

Where a block is separated from the plateau by erosion it becomes a **mesa**. The steep faces have a scree slope at the break of slope. This eroded material is carried away and is replaced by more eroded material keeping the free face and the scree slope constant in angle.

When a mesa is eroded away so that its width is less than the height it becomes a **butte**. These incredible formations are found in places like Monument Valley and Bryce Canyon.

There are several resistant **volcanic necks** which stand proud of the landscape. The most famous of these is the 550m Ship Rock with its radial dykes.

Figure 2.9

21

'...As a navigable stream it possesses some advantages during the dry season; boats can seldom sink in it; and for the matter of channels it has an unusual variety. The main channel shifts so often that the most skilful pilot always knows where it is not to be found by pursuing the course of his last trip...'
J Ross Browne, 1864.

There is no doubt that the Colorado Basin is one of the most spectacular areas of scenery in the whole of North America. Evidence of this in the present time lies in the number of National Parks, National Monuments, National Recreation Areas and National Forests found within its drainage basin. At the same time it is a landscape which poses great problems for human survival. The climatic problems have already been mentioned and in the past the great canyons have acted as barriers to movement and served as a disincentive for early settlement.

The Indian tribes like Hohokam, Anasazi, and Mogollon dating back to 1000 BC realised very early on that controlling the Colorado was the key to any development of the south west. Small areas of the south west desert were able to support communities of up to 5000 people. Using a complex series of irrigation ditches and channels they were able to grow crops of maize, squash and beans. These civilizations survived till 1130 AD when their rain-making rituals failed to relieve a cycle of drought which forced them to leave these lands.

According to one author, the Colorado has been ingrained in the American psyche as a symbol of the promise and the problems of the west. The river indeed did pose great problems. Its flow was extremely unreliable. Some of its tributaries were reduced to dried up river beds at certain times of the year and at other times they and the Colorado could become a raging torrent as sudden flash floods carried down thousands of tonnes of sediment clearing everything in their path. In a desert environment a riverside location was not always the safest place to settle and near the Gulf of California the river often changed course with disastrous effects. The river, charged up with sediment, built up its bed until it was flowing along a channel several metres above the surrounding area and when the flow increased periodically it just broke its banks and flowed down some other channel until the cycle repeated itself.

Some of these problems can be seen in figure 2.10.

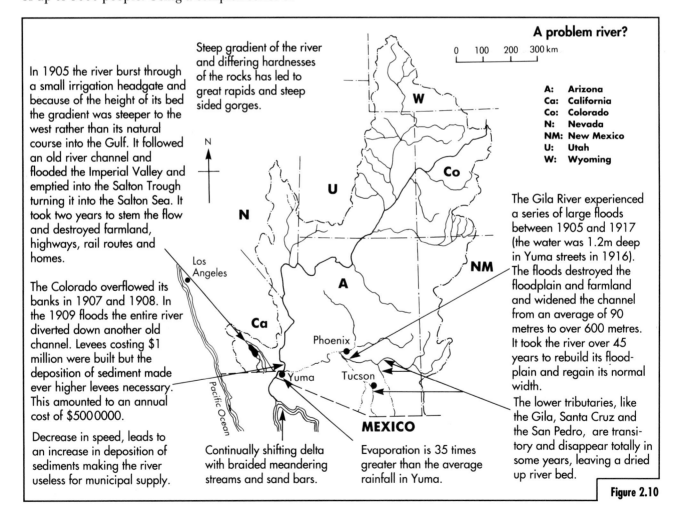

A problem river?

In 1905 the river burst through a small irrigation headgate and because of the height of its bed the gradient was steeper to the west rather than its natural course into the Gulf. It followed an old river channel and flooded the Imperial Valley and emptied into the Salton Trough turning it into the Salton Sea. It took two years to stem the flow and destroyed farmland, highways, rail routes and homes.

The Colorado overflowed its banks in 1907 and 1908. In the 1909 floods the entire river diverted down another old channel. Levees costing $1 million were built but the deposition of sediment made ever higher levees necessary. This amounted to an annual cost of $500 000.

Decrease in speed, leads to an increase in deposition of sediments making the river useless for municipal supply.

Steep gradient of the river and differing hardnesses of the rocks has led to great rapids and steep sided gorges.

Continually shifting delta with braided meandering streams and sand bars.

0 100 200 300 km

A: Arizona
Ca: California
Co: Colorado
N: Nevada
NM: New Mexico
U: Utah
W: Wyoming

The Gila River experienced a series of large floods between 1905 and 1917 (the water was 1.2m deep in Yuma streets in 1916). The floods destroyed the floodplain and farmland and widened the channel from an average of 90 metres to over 600 metres. It took the river over 45 years to rebuild its flood-plain and regain its normal width.

The lower tributaries, like the Gila, Santa Cruz and the San Pedro, are transitory and disappear totally in some years, leaving a dried up river bed.

Evaporation is 35 times greater than the average rainfall in Yuma.

Figure 2.10

11 Describe the major physical and climatic features of the Colorado Basin which makes settlement difficult.

12 What problems do farmers face as a result of the annual discharge pattern?

13 Refer to an atlas map of precipitation averages for North America. How true is the saying '... the east is wet and the west is dry ...'

14 With the help of an atlas, try to explain why there is such a huge regional variation in precipitation. Mention should be made of onshore winds, distance from the sea, rain shadow and evaporation.

15 What climatic reasons account for this 'difficult landscape' having the fastest growing population in the USA?

16 Identify some of the major physical problems in controlling a river like the Colorado.

Control or Subjugation?

'...Water resource projects have many positive environmental effects. When water management practices regulate and augment low flows of rivers, decrease erosion, prevent floods, eliminate waste of water, and in many instances, change deserts into gardens where man can comfortably live and prosper, the result is a betterment of environmental conditions...'

Gilbert Stamm (former commissioner of US Bureau of Reclamation)

Uncontrolled and unregulated the Colorado had limited value. The yearly threat of floods or drought made large irrigation projects uncertain, and the heavy load of sediment carried downstream by the river made it totally unsuitable for a public water supply. Without regulation and control of its floodplain there could be no expansion of irrigated farmland. Faced with this problem and seeing that the power of the river could not be controlled on a local basis, the people of the south west turned to the federal authorities. The solution was simple in theory. All that had to be done was to build a large dam, or series of dams, which would store water when there was an excess and release it when there was a shortage. There were plenty of ideal sites in the narrow but deep gorges in the north and the water could also be used to produce hydro-electricity, which could pay for the huge construction costs and help pump the water to its final destination if it happened to be higher than the dam site.

WATER ALLOCATION

Before the work could start, the problem of river allocation had to be sorted out. The river basin included areas of seven states, all with differing agricultural, industrial and public needs. Water rights in America is a very complex issue. The system in most states for rights to water was similar to that in operation for land. If a settler could lay claim to a piece of land and prove that it was being properly used, then that land became the property of the settler. With water, this system of 'prior appropriation' meant that if one state built a dam and diverted huge amounts of water for some irrigation scheme then the other states would have no comeback. Theoretically another state could not, at a later stage, build another dam if the water taken from the river deprived the earlier scheme. This legal system obviously worked in favour of the state of California. It had the financial means and, because of its rapidly growing population and industries, the desire to avail itself of a regular water supply from the Colorado. The other states realised that a major flood control scheme was desirable and inevitable but they were understandably worried about water running through their states and ending up benefiting the economy of California.

COLORADO COMPACT

In 1922, after two years of discussion and debate, a compact was signed by six of the states. The compromise which led to eventual agreement allowed for the division of the basin into two separate units; the Upper Colorado and the Lower Colorado. The exact amount each state would get was to be decided at a later date. This would allow California to start work on a major scheme to control the river and at the same time guarantee that there would be enough water left for the other states to develop and make use of, when their economies and population growth demanded it. The compact became effective in 1929 after the government, with the approval of the six ratifying states, passed an act dividing the Colorado. In a separate act, California agreed not to exceed a strict limit of 5.4km^3 out of a total of 9.25km^3 allocated to the lower basin plus not more than half of any unused water. The division of the water within the lower basin was eventually decided by a ruling of the Supreme Court in 1963. The upper basin states reached agreement in a 1948 compact. They had also learned from the arguments within the lower basin states and they allocated a percentage of the water available, rather than an absolute volume of a variable amount.

WATER AVAILABILITY

The division can be seen in figure 2.11 and shows that California, as a result of its greater population and political muscle, managed to gain the largest proportion of the water. This is in spite of the fact that 83 per cent of the water from the Colorado actually has its origin in the upper basin.

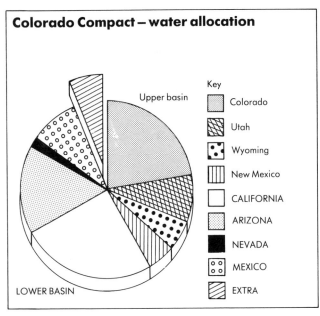

Colorado Compact – water allocation

Key
- Colorado
- Utah
- Wyoming
- New Mexico
- CALIFORNIA
- ARIZONA
- NEVADA
- MEXICO
- EXTRA

Upper basin

LOWER BASIN

Figure 2.11

Unfortunately, rivers do not always follow such a strict budgeting procedure and because of the great climatic variability within the basin, the annual flow, so neatly divided by the basin states, is one of the most disputed hydrological records in the USA. Since the early 1920s there has been a downturn in the amount of water actually flowing into the river and therefore available for storage and diversion. Estimates of the long term annual flows vary from 14.5km^3 to 20.7km^3 depending on the time period selected. One expert estimated that the average annual figure could be as low as 13.5km^3. The basic problem is that the river is, in theory, supposed to be able to produce 18.5km^3 per year to satisfy the allocations decided in the various compacts and statutes together known as the 'Law of the River'. The upper basin is also legally bound to supply 92.5km^3 every ten years to the lower basin. If the water in the river is below average, then the lower basin is entitled to a bigger share of less water.

This leaves the upper basin in a difficult situation. Should they set up water projects to make use of their water entitlements, knowing that in some years, because of the Law of the River, supplies will not always be guaranteed?

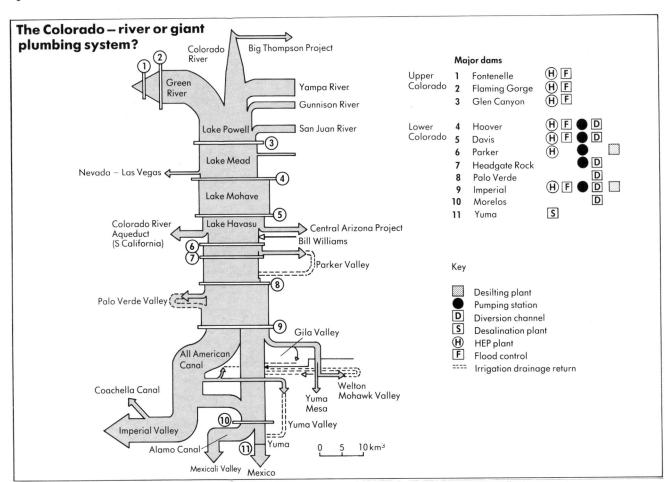

The Colorado – river or giant plumbing system?

	Major dams		
Upper Colorado	1	Fontenelle	H F
	2	Flaming Gorge	H F
	3	Glen Canyon	H F
Lower Colorado	4	Hoover	H F ● D
	5	Davis	H F ● D
	6	Parker	H ● ▦
	7	Headgate Rock	● D
	8	Palo Verde	D
	9	Imperial	H F ● D ▦
	10	Morelos	D
	11	Yuma	S

Key
- ▦ Desilting plant
- ● Pumping station
- D Diversion channel
- S Desalination plant
- H HEP plant
- F Flood control
- ===== Irrigation drainage return

Colorado River
Big Thompson Project
Green River
Yampa River
Gunnison River
San Juan River
Lake Powell
Lake Mead
Nevada – Las Vegas
Lake Mohave
Colorado River Aqueduct (S California)
Lake Havasu
Central Arizona Project
Bill Williams
Parker Valley
Palo Verde Valley
Gila Valley
All American Canal
Coachella Canal
Welton Mohawk Valley
Yuma Mesa
Yuma Valley
Imperial Valley
Yuma
Alamo Canal
Mexicali Valley
Mexico

0   5   10 km^3

Figure 2.12

CONTROLLING THE RIVER

*'...As an engineer, I fully appreciate the magnificent
structures that have brought the Lower Colorado under
control, but I confess that I have the same sympathy for my
old friend, the sometimes wayward, but always interesting,
and still unconquered and untrammelled river that I have
for a bird in a cage, or an animal in a zoo...'*
Godfrey Sykes

If someone were to write a DIY guide to shaping
the natural environment, destroying an ancient and
fragile landscape, using up scarce resources and
funding it all with government money, then the
author would have to look no further than the
Colorado. Developers, engineers and politicians have
combined to spend billions of taxpayers dollars in
building huge dams, moving billions of cubic metres
of water to supply a few farmers who grow products
which in many cases nobody wants, adding to the
surpluses of crops which could be grown cheaper in
the east and with little damage to the environment.

As can be seen in figure 2.12 the Colorado is
probably the most carefully managed river system in
the world. Although the original aim of the first
major dam (Hoover) was to ensure flood protection,
it can be seen now as a multi-purpose scheme
embodying water supply for irrigation, large cities,
and industries, the generation of huge amounts of
hydro-electricity, and supporting a growing demand
for water based recreation in a desert landscape. The
area involved has the greatest water deficiency of any
in the USA, but more water is exported out of the
river basin than any other in America.

17 Why was control over the river essential before any
real development could take place?
18 Prior appropriation could be described as 'first
come, first served'. Who benefitted most from this
system and why?
19 Why do you think it took so long for the states to
decide on the amount of water each area should
get?
20 With reference to figure 2.12 describe the major
differences between the upper and the lower basin
river systems.
21 Explain why the lower basin will benefit most if the
flow of the river is lower than average for a few
years.

Multi-purpose Benefits

In any major multi-purpose scheme like that on the
Colorado there are numerous benefits but at the
same time there are usually associated problems
because of the scale of the operations, the level of
control over an extremely variable hydrological
cycle and the balance which has to be achieved
between the use and abuse of a fragile environment.
In the case of the Colorado, the river has been so
tightly regulated, variable water flows over used and
accounted for in such a way as to cause real management and financial problems in its future allocation
and quality control.

FLOOD CONTROL

The Bureau of Reclamation in one of its publications
states that 'flood control does not mean flood
prevention' and that downstream areas 'are less
likely to be flooded'. This is not really an escape
clause but an acceptance that the control of the vast
forces of the weather and the river itself is not always
possible. The 'El Nino' floods of 1983 with the
highest recorded flows in history are a good example
of the fragile control people have over the river. A
mixture of extreme weather conditions, poor
weather forecasting and the failure of the bureau to
release water soon enough to make space to store the
flood waters caused millions of dollars worth of
damage to farm land and property especially in the
Parker Valley. Here local county planning
departments had sanctioned the building of a row of
holiday residences along the shores of the river on
the floodplain. They were perhaps fooled by the
long filling period of Lake Mead and Lake Powell
(1962-1980) into thinking that the great variability of
precipitation of the area had been finally controlled
by the immense structures upstream. Many experts
at the time felt that the bureau was responsible
because of its water storage policy. The upper basin
releases the minimum amounts which the lower
basin is legally entitled to, and at the same time the
Bureau of Reclamation policy is to hold as much
water as possible in reserve in case of a period of
drought. This policy seems to go against the original
aims of the dams, ie drought is a greater concern
than a particularly wet year leading to flood hazards.
Although not officially admitted, higher water levels
also maximise power production and ensure greater
revenues from its sale. A study by the General
Accounting Office after the 1983 floods predicted
that if the river continued to be managed with its
reservoirs full or nearly full, controlled flooding
could be expected to occur once every 10 to 15 years.

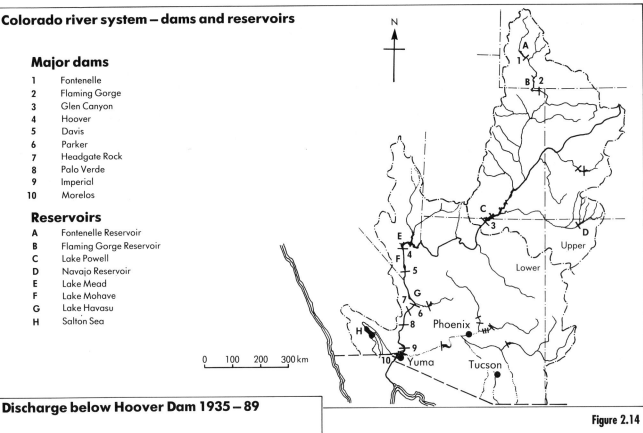

Colorado river system – dams and reservoirs

Major dams

1	Fontenelle
2	Flaming Gorge
3	Glen Canyon
4	Hoover
5	Davis
6	Parker
7	Headgate Rock
8	Palo Verde
9	Imperial
10	Morelos

Reservoirs

A	Fontenelle Reservoir
B	Flaming Gorge Reservoir
C	Lake Powell
D	Navajo Reservoir
E	Lake Mead
F	Lake Mohave
G	Lake Havasu
H	Salton Sea

0 100 200 300 km

Figure 2.14

Discharge below Hoover Dam 1935 – 89

Hoover Dam completed
Fill of Lake Mead

Glen Canyon Dam
Filling of Lake Powell

Figure 2.13

In any river management system the variability of the climatic system can lead to problems at both ends of any unpredictability scale. In this case both drought and flooding have been evident over hundreds of years but the whole control system breaks down if the balance of how much water to store and how much to release is not properly addressed. As can be seen in figure 2.13, the bureau has been able to regulate the flow of the river fairly well and there is no doubt that the damage during 1983 would have been much worse without the upstream storage reservoirs.

POWER

Originally the intention in building the major dams was to control variable water supply. The hydro-electric power potential was seen as a means of paying back their massive construction costs, but since then it has been seen as an end in itself and it has helped stimulate the development of the area with a ready source of cheap power. The reservoirs are managed so that the levels are kept as high as possible for as long as possible to guarantee the maximum amount of head for the generators. Dams like the Hoover, Davis, Parker and Glen Canyon produce an incredible amount of electricity. In 1990 Hoover Dam produced 4 billion kw hours of electricity. This is enough to supply 500 000 homes. Glen Canyon HEP pays for 85 per cent of the cost of providing water to the farmers of the upper basin. Some of the power is used to pump irrigation water. The Parker Dam for instance, uses half of its output to pump water along the Colorado Aqueduct to the farms in southern California and the city of San Diego. This is no mean feat as the water has to be lifted a total of 1000 metres over the Tehachapi Range. The Central Arizona Project water sent along the Granite Reef Aqueduct to Phoenix and the Gila Salt Aqueduct to Tucson has to be lifted 300 metres and then a further 25 metres before it reaches its final destination.

RECREATION

The reservoirs are a great boon to the tourist industry. Lakes Mead, Parker and Havasu have created a major recreational area in an arid region where large natural bodies of water are non existent. Fishing, boating, swimming and water skiing are enjoyed by millions of visitors. Caravan sites, trailer parks, cabins and picnic sites are situated along their shores. Lake Mead has six marinas with a full range of ancillary services which attract more than 8 million visitors. Lake Havasu city is also the home of London Bridge and is a major tourist attraction. Fingers of desert jutting out into the reservoirs act as beaches, which are popular in the searing heat of the summer. The dams themselves attract a great number of tourists and Hoover has a visitor centre attracting more than 700 000 visitors annually.

AGRICULTURE

There is no doubt that the prime beneficiaries of the billions of dollars spent since the 1930s have been the farmers of the area. The west uses nine times more irrigation water than the east (see figure 2.15) and most of this has been heavily subsidised. A great variety of crops are grown, from low value (74 per cent) alfalfa used for fodder to high value (9 per cent) citrus crops and market vegetables. One expert estimates that 45 per cent of the crops grown under irrigation are crops which are surplus in the USA. The Reclamation Act in 1902 which set up the bureau, was originally empowered to help small farmers but in actual fact, very few farmers benefit from the massive injection of federal funds. Bud Antle is one of these large commercial farms. It produces lettuce and celery on irrigated farmland occupying 80 square kilometres. The Imperial Valley is the largest area of irrigated land in the western hemisphere.

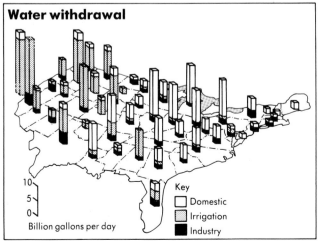

Water withdrawal

10
5
0
Billion gallons per day

Key
Domestic
Irrigation
Industry

MUNICIPAL WATER SUPPLY

The water carried by canals like the Colorado Aqueduct (Los Angeles), San Diego Aqueduct (San Diego) the Robert Griffith Project (Las Vegas) and the Central Arizona Project (Tucson, Phoenix) have helped satisfy rising municipal demand for supplies of domestic water in an area of limited and extremely variable rainfall. The high temperatures of the area are indicated by the domestic water uses in these rapidly growing cities. The highest figures are for lawn irrigation, swimming pools and evaporative cooling.

INDUSTRY

Industry is another sector which benefits from the cheap, pollution free source of power. The mining and mineral industries using hydro-electricity include borax, tungsten, cement, aluminium, salt and steel in California; manganese, silica sand in Nevada and the low cost energy helped revitalise the copper industry in Arizona. Another important factor in hydro-electricity generation is that of resource conservation. It would take 6 million barrels per annum of ever more expensive oil to produce the electricity generated by Hoover Dam alone.

WILDLIFE

The huge artificial lakes act as sanctuaries for waterfowl such as the pintail, mallard, snow goose, and waders like the egret and blue heron. More than 250 species of birds have been counted within the Lake Mead National Recreation Area.

SEDIMENT CONTROL

Engineers estimated that at one time the River Colorado carried 266 tonnes of sand and sediment through the Grand Canyon every minute. The Hoover Dam acts as a giant trap for this sediment and the newer Glen Canyon Dam now retains 75 per cent of the sediment which used to flow into Lake Mead. In the upper basin several other smaller dams perform similar functions on the tributaries. In the lower basin the Imperial Dam also has desilting facilities. The silt is collected in a settling basin before it is dredged out and dumped on land.

Figure 2.15

27

22 What do you think has been the major benefit from the control of the River Colorado? Give your reasons.
23 Why did the 'El Nino' floods of 1983 cause so much damage?
24 Explain why the floods of 1983 showed up the problems of river basin management in an area of rainfall variability.
25 Why would the Bureau of Reclamation still claim success for their policies of flood control?
26 Describe what has been done to lessen the problems caused by silting up of the storage reservoirs.
27 Describe some of the conflicts involved in water management on such a huge scale.
28 Why do so many western states use so much irrigation water?
29 Explain why the creation of hydro-electricity was so essential when building these large dams.

Problems to be Solved

Despite the obvious benefits ensuing from the control of the River Colorado there are many problems still to be overcome. Many of these are a direct result of human interference in the fragile balance of a desert landscape.

SALINITY

In its virgin state the Colorado always carried salts estimated to be in the region of 6 million tonnes per year. This came from exposed saline shale formations and from springs in the upper basin. With the control of the river and the increase in irrigated farm land the amounts of salts carried in solution has risen tremendously. Farmers applying huge amounts of water to their fields, leach salts out of the soils and into the drainage water which returns higher and higher concentrations of salt into the river. This concentration is increased when water is stored in the reservoirs because of the effect of evaporation. The Colorado entering the Grand Valley has 200 parts per million (ppm) salt and by the time it has been returned after irrigation use this has risen to 6500ppm. Farmers downstream faced with saline water have to use excessive amounts to ensure that their crops survive or have to change to a low yielding crop which is more salt resistant. The problem of saline soils is increased by the upward movement of water containing soluble salts due to capillary action and evaporation. Salinisation has forced many farmers to give up their irrigated land or they have been bought out by the Bureau of Reclamation. It is much cheaper for the bureau to buy out the farmers rather than contemplate spending millions of dollars trying to build underground drains to carry away the salty drainage water only for it to end up in the river again and push the problem somewhere further downstream. One good example is the Wellton Mohawk area, on the Gila River in Arizona, which drains into the Colorado just north of the international border with Mexico. The Mexicans watched helplessly as their river water became increasingly saline (from 400mg/l at the beginning of this century to 800mg/l at the current time). Crop yield losses begin when the salt concentrations reach 700 to 850mg/l depending on soil conditions and crop type. The Americans contended that they were still supplying the agreed amount of water and that they had not said anything about the quality of the water. After discussions in 1973, the USA agreed to build a huge desalinisation plant at Yuma to clean up the Colorado River before it entered Mexico and thus safeguarding the irrigated farm land of the Mexicali valley, the most fertile area in Mexico. This $300 million plant, opened in 1992 nine years behind schedule, has annual running costs of $20 million. The total cost of salinisation is more than $113 million and this is expected to double by 2010 AD if no action is taken. Municipal, commercial and industrial users suffer the corrosive action of salinity on plumbing and industrial boilers and are faced with increasing costs for water treatment.

Figure 2.16

Water loss

Steep sides and narrow gorge profiles were physically ideal for building large dams and producing huge storage reservoirs with limited surface areas. Unfortunately many of these large reservoirs lose millions of cubic metres every year through evaporation. Lake Powell loses $0.74km^3$ with the average annual loss of the whole river amounting to $2.4km^3$ annually during 1975-80.

A large amount of water is also lost every year through seepage. In the Navajo reservoir the situation was so bad that the Bureau of Reclamation had to build a cut-off wall (opened in 1988) to reduce this seepage. Lake Powell, with massive horizontal layers of sandstone along its banks also suffers from this problem. It is estimated that the $300km^3$ lake loses $1.25km^3$ annually. The builders knew that this would happen but hoped that the soluble salts in the water would eventually plug the gaps and stop the wastage. Every year the capacity of reservoirs like Lake Mead and Lake Powell is reduced because of the deposition of silt. Lake Powell loses $86\,000m^3$ of space every year because of silt displacement.

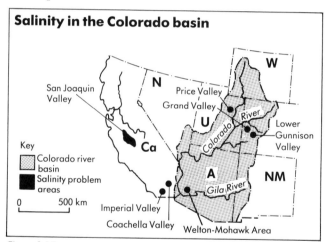

Salinity in the Colorado basin

Figure 2.17

30 What is the point being made by the cartoon in figure 2.16?

31 Explain how the Colorado River becomes more saline as it moves downstream. Refer to figure 2.12.

32 Why have the Mexicans good reason to be annoyed with the Bureau of Reclamation?

33 Why was a new desalination plant built at Yuma?

34 The 'ecosystem' approach to salinity might be to buy the farmers out and stop irrigating those areas with known saline deposits. Describe what has been seen as the 'plumbing system approach'.

35 'Salinity is just a farmers problem'. How true is this statement?

Groundwater overdraft

Figure 2.18 shows all the states where 25 per cent or more of their water used comes from groundwater sources. It can be seen that the west, and the Colorado in particular, rely heavily on groundwater sources. In some areas of Arizona more than 85 per cent of withdrawals are from underground and this groundwater mining is in many cases in excess of groundwater recharge leading to groundwater 'overdraft'. This has led to a drop in water table levels and, in some areas, to major subsidence.

This use of underground water is understandable when experts talk of the top 30 metres of rocks containing amounts up to $8km^3$ which is four times the surface storage of reservoirs in the region.

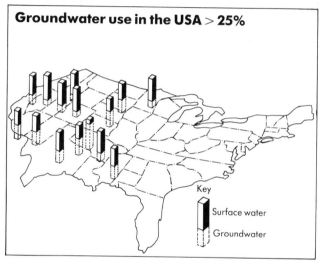

Groundwater use in the USA > 25%

Key
Surface water
Groundwater

Figure 2.18

Water waste

Farmers use the majority of the water in the arid west. Figure 2.18 shows that in the states of the Colorado basin, irrigated farm land uses 90 per cent of the water. The farmers in the Colorado generally pay well below the going price for this irrigation water. The World Resources Institute estimated that the average effective subsidy for the 140 different agricultural projects amounted to 83 per cent of their cost and that the total subsidy amounted to $1billion per year. The price the farmers have to pay is based on their ability to pay. It is estimated that 45 per cent of the land that is irrigated in the west is growing crops officially in surplus. In the desert some farmers paying $3.50 per acre foot for water which costs the bureau some $300 per acre foot to supply, are using the cheap water to grow thirsty rice crops. In Louisiana and Arkansas farmers are being paid NOT to grow rice to prevent a commodity price collapse. Until recently there was no advantage in a farmer saving water. By law the farmers were not allowed to store it until the following year, nor were they allowed to sell it to a thirsty urban settlement. They could use it or lose it. There is little incentive to use some of the more modern techniques like laser levelling, drip irrigation or even to line the irrigation channels to prevent seepage. Channel seepage loses one-third of all water diverted for irrigation. A farmer using flood irrigation will generally use twice as much water as the crop would actually need if the water supply was properly managed.

Figure 2.19

WATER POLITICS

Water resource management in the Colorado, still has a lot more to do with politics rather than proper management of a scarce resource. Any objective study of the projects sanctioned and built would have to admit that environmental impact, proper accounting control and realistic costing were not treated as seriously as were, what has been termed, 'pork barrel politics'. Senators and congressmen in the western states see water projects as bringing real 'kudos' as well as good publicity. One cynical author once wrote that a 'good scheme' was worth four or five elections; getting the bill passed, land purchase, digging the first sod, and cutting the ribbon at its opening. It is the promise which counts. A politician supporting a new scheme can attract the votes of the farmers, estate agents, construction workers, even the unemployed looking for a job. Never mind the economics of a scheme which might use more power than it would ever produce through hydro-electricity or one that might flood more land than will be irrigated. It has been shown that the Bureau of Reclamation has been 'economical with the truth' when costings for potential projects have been published.

J McCaull in an article 'Dams of Pork' reported on instances where sponsoring agencies, intent on having their project authorised, overstated expected annual monetary gains to be realised from flood control, irrigation, hydro-elctricity and outdoor recreation. They underestimated the annual costs for maintenance and operation, reservoir flooding and loss of outdoor recreation sites.

In some schemes costing $100 million, less than 100 farmers have actually benefited. This does not stand up as a sensible, logical use of scarce finances and even scarcer water.

ENVIRONMENTAL DAMAGE

In all the brochures produced by the Bureau of Reclamation there are sections stating how the reservoirs are ideal sanctuaries for certain bird and fish. Nowhere is there any mention of the actual environmental damage done by the dams and associated reservoirs. Many people believe that a great natural wildscape has been destroyed. There used to be beavers in Tucson, but the river has now dried up. There used to be a great variety of birdlife in the Colorado delta but this is now a total wasteland and salt desert.

Rainbow Bridge is one of the great geological wonders of the world. Despite government assurances the bureau has kept the level of Lake Powell so high, to maximise HEP production, that the waters of the reservoir are slowly dissolving this great natural monument. Thousands of animals and birds have been drowned or shifted by reservoir flooding like that at Lake Mead and Lake Powell. Some farmers and politicians still see the Grand Canyon as a potential reservoir.

36 What are the main climatic reasons for Arizona having to use so much water from underground sources?

37 What are the major consequences of groundwater overdraft in the Colorado Basin?

38 Some would say that cheap water pricing has been the main factor in the spread of farming in the area. Explain why this policy has led to 'water waste'.

39 What could farmers do to save water and why do they not do it?

40 Why have so many large projects been constructed sometimes at the expense of smaller but more environmentally friendly schemes?

Future Management Issues

The history of river management has, in some senses, now turned full circle. Controlling the river was a means to an end, a way of conquering the desert and taming a wild environment. Huge dams were built, canals carried water uphill, through mountain ranges, along underground pipelines, and reservoirs have been created covering hundreds of square kilometres. The last great monument of the Bureau of Reclamation will probably be the Central Arizona Project.

CENTRAL ARIZONA PROJECT (CAP)

"Of course I was for it. Any Arizona politician who wanted any kind of political future had to be for it. If I had voted against it I would probably have been shot".

Sam Steiger, former Congressman

This $3.6 billion scheme, planned for completion in 1992, will carry water 500km across the desert from Lake Havasu to the major urban areas around Phoenix and Tucson. The scheme has been in the planning or law court stage for more than 50 years. It is a scheme originally designed to allow farmers to continue growing crops in the desert in areas where land has already gone out of production due to lack of water or the effects of salinisation. This area is, on present usage, so short of water it has been groundwater mining since 1940 (see figure 2.20) Even when this water, promised to Arizona under the Colorado Compact in 1922 arrives, groundwater use will only be cut by 60 per cent. State plans to cut groundwater mining by 2025 AD look very fragile, based on current population growth rates. The population of the Tucson area is expected to more than double from 0.62 million in 1986 to 1.59 million by 2025.

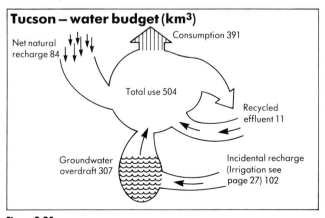

Figure 2.20

This CAP water has, up till 1987, travelled towards southern California along the Colorado Aqueduct. Under a legal agreement the amount sent to Arizona increased gradually until 1992 while the amount sent to the metropolitan water district of southern California gradually decreased.

THE ENVIRONMENT FIGHTS BACK

There is little doubt that the Bureau of Reclamation will not be able to squeeze any more out of the Colorado for three reasons.

Environmental lobby

By the 1960s less than 2 per cent of the United States had wilderness characteristics and this made many people realise that this too, could disappear. Many of the most recent water schemes have been abandoned because the increasingly powerful environmental movement, such as the 'High Sierra Club' in California, have been able to get public opinion on their side and reject the idea that the Colorado needs even more dams and storage reservoirs. Lengthy court battles and public referendums have forestalled planned developments.

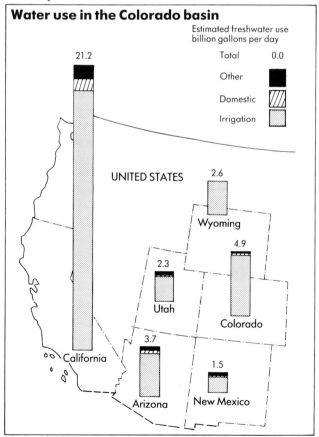

Figure 2.21

31

Realistic water pricing

In the Colorado Basin states, farmers use up to 92 per cent of the water from the river and groundwater sources (see figure 2.21) They have received this water at vastly subsidised prices. In one scheme costing $931 million, only 5 per cent had been paid back after 40 years. In 1987 a new regulation was passed stating that in any new schemes the farmers had to pay the full cost of the water and that each state had to pay half of the cost of the full project.

If this act had been passed 30 years earlier, many projects just would not have got past the drawing board. The upper basin states have set in motion several totally uneconomic schemes because they were desperate to find a way to use their water. If they had been paying for it, rather than the Government, through the Bureau of Reclamation, then most of these schemes would have been difficult to justify.

Engineering problems

There is no doubt that the 'best sites' have been used up. Geological problems, combined with ever increasing costs, in reality means the end of the grandiose schemes in the Colorado and elsewhere in the 'west'. One small scheme on a small river in California was forecast to cost as much as NASA paid to send one man to the moon!

41 In what ways will developers have to take a more realistic view about the viability of future projects?
42 What would be the simplest ways of solving water shortages in some of the largest cities?
43 Describe the ways the farmers could be persuaded to use less water.
44 Describe the measures taken by some states to reduce the demand for water.
45 What are water markets and what are their main advantages?
46 In what ways could the use of groundwater be described as another example of the 'plumbing system approach'?

THE FUTURE

There is a real lack of interstate institutions responsible for basin wide management and the numerous problems of water supply, division and quality present a real challenge for the seven states to find opportunities to co-operate and maximise benefits from the available resources.

Several recent studies have put forward alternative ways of managing the water within the basin, both above and below ground. Some of these policies are already being tried out in a piecemeal fashion by different states but so far there has been no real attempt to formalise any scheme to look at water conservation over the whole of the Colorado Basin.

Restricting demand by restructuring the pricing system

A trip around many cities would reveal hundreds of private swimming pools with lawn sprinklers whirring away unattended. In the drought period from 1985–91 such residents have been legally forced to reduce the amount of water they use. In Santa Barbara, California, lawn watering has been banned and drought officers prowl the streets looking for offenders with the power to make a $250 spot fine. In Glendale, Arizona, households are given rebates for fitting automatic sprinkler controls and installing water saving toilets. Residents in cities in Colorado and Arizona are given tax credits if they use sensible garden landscaping. This basically means planting arid-adaptive plants, using Mexican paving stone and in some cases using a green painted stone mulch. This has been spurred on by hefty price increases which are very important in an area where 50 per cent of the water bill will go towards landscape irrigation. The water being delivered to central Arizona will cost about $250 per acre foot, while users will only be expected to pay $58. In southern California, which is having its water supply from the Colorado decreased with the advent of the CAP, the water authorities have tried price rises to help cut water use. It was found that a 12 per cent rise led to a 10 per cent drop in per capita use. Farmers using 90 per cent of California's water have been forced (February 1991) to cut their water use by 75 per cent and urban dwellers will only get between 25 and 50 per cent of their normal allocation. Many experts believe that these policies should be used all the time and not just as a short term answer to a period of drought.

Reallocation of water between users

Water markets
With agriculture using the vast majority of the water it would seem logical to transfer some of their water to urban uses. In California a 10 per cent drop in irrigation of farm land would enable the cities to double the amount of water available. The major problem in water transfer is the legal restrictions on water sale. Technically land is sold with its water rights. In most states water cannot be sold on its

own. Tucson has bought up agricultural land in Avra Valley to the west of the city. Phoenix and its suburb of Scottsdale have done likewise, buying up farm land in remote areas of western Arizona, which by law they must continue to farm until the water rights can be legally transferred to municipal use. They then plan to use the CAP canal to bring the water to the city. This increase in water marketing has led to half of the water rights in the Gila area of Arizona being transferred to municipal uses. There is no doubt that with the increasing power of the cities this movement should be encouraged and the marketing made easier in other states by a change in the legal frameworks and institutions so that it can be managed in a more organised fashion.

Conservation

Some conservation measures always appear during periods of drought but many people feel that these measures should be actively encouraged all the time and extended into all areas. Farmers, for instance, have no real incentive to save water. If they pay a lot of money for an expensive laser levelling of their fields or line their ditches with concrete to stop seepage, or set up a drip irrigation system using 10 per cent of the water they would use in flood irrigation, what benefits do they gain? They have not been able to sell water or even store it because of the archaic water rights legislation. It is either 'use it or lose it'. Some politicians are now looking at ways in which farmers could benefit from any savings they might make. If the legal framework was altered alongside tax incentives to encourage water conservation measures, then there would be plenty of water to go around and satisfy all potential population and industrial growth. In one of the most publicised examples of this, the metropolitan water district of southern California is paying for the concrete lining of irrigation ditches in the Imperial Valley. The water saved will travel along the All-American Canal to the thirsty cities like Los Angeles and San Diego.

Improving the use of groundwater resources

Advances in groundwater hydrology have made the use of this great resource much more possible, but a balance has to be attained between the use of river water and the underground aquifers which have taken millions of years to form. Research is being carried out and in some test sites, scientists have been able to recharge the underground aquifers using one of two methods (see figure 2.22). In any year of excess surface water, it might be possible to place some of it underground, cutting down on evaporation loss and in some areas helping to push back the salty water which is working its way closer to the surface with the increase in groundwater mining.

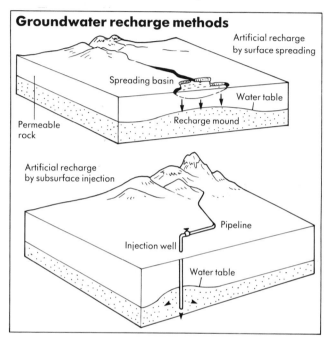

Figure 2.22

SUMMARY

- Even full mobility of water supplies and much more efficient water use cannot change the fact that the west is a desert or close to it.
- The best cure for a threatening water shortage is not necessarily more water; savings in water use, or transfer of water use to less consumptive, higher yield applications or discovery of new techniques of water management may offer better solutions.

3 TOWARDS AN ECOSYSTEM APPROACH

The feasibility of feeding the predicted five fold population increase in Africa and a doubling of numbers in Asia - two continents at present crippled by land degradation and widespread malnutrition - depends on the successful restoration and conservation of soil productivity. Large areas of the aptly named 'hunger zone' (figure 3.1) are locked in a vicious circle of degradation (figure 3.2) due to:

- mismanagement of land because of problems of over population, poor soils, use of marginal lands and fuelwood harvesting
- degradation caused by destruction of the vegetation cover leading to rapid surface runoff and soil erosion. Badly planned and operated irrigation schemes also add to the problem.

To secure the conservation of land and water resources this vicious circle must be reversed (see figure 3.3). Many ecologists do not believe this is possible unless an ecosystem approach is adopted to find solutions to the problems.

In the past water has been regarded as a commodity to be controlled and supplied. The inevitable side effects of controls seemed to come as a surprise rather than being considered and action planned. The beneficial use of the water cycle is seldom possible without some manipulation or regulation of the system and the inevitable negative side effects should be recognised, quantified, and balanced against the intended benefits (figure 3.4). In this particular trade-off, water appears on both sides - as a source of food and energy, and as an agent of negative side effects.

ENGINEERING APPROACH

The traditional approach to water management in an area or country is to compare the potential water availability of the area, as measured by the long term average river runoff, with the water requirements for different water supply purposes. Very little water loss is admitted, water use efficiency is invariably overestimated and problems from the negative side effects of dams are dealt with as and when they arise. Occasionally this is not possible.

Although this engineering approach has proved more than adequate in Western Europe and North America, it has been found wanting in developing regions where plant production is severely restricted by chronic water shortages. Indeed the resulting ineffectiveness of river basin planning in addressing major social, economic and environmental issues in the Developing World has led to numerous campaigns against river planning projects by the very people the planners claim to be helping. For instance, a successful campaign was waged by the residents of Chico Valley in The Philippines in order to save their homelands (figure 3.5), and more recently efforts of 100 000 peasants in western India, who were about to be displaced by a dam on the River Narmada, have managed to force the World Bank to have second thoughts. A cynical view is that the major beneficiaries of every large scheme built so far in the Developing World has been overseas construction and consultancy firms.

The water cycle defines water availability, which in turn controls the agricultural output of a given area. It follows that water places definite limits on the number of people an ecosystem can support on a self-reliant basis. This limit is referred to as a system's 'carrying capacity' which could be used to adopt an ecologically based approach to water management problems, especially in periods of water scarcity.

The carrying capacity obviously varies from region to region. Under optimal conditions around 500mm of water on one hectare of cultivated land would be necessary to support a population of four people and two cattle. This amount corresponds to 1250 cubic metres per person per year - a figure which could be used to calculate the water requirements of an area from an ecological aspect.

A projection of the increasing water competition which will take place over the next century is shown in figure 3.6. By far the greatest changes will affect Asia and Africa. Water availability on a per capita basis in Asia will be halved from 5100 to 2600 cubic metres per person. In Africa the figure will be reduced from 9000 to 1600 cubic metres per person.

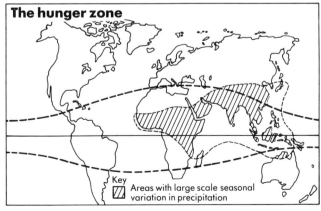

The hunger zone

Key
▨ Areas with large scale seasonal variation in precipitation

Figure 3.1

Vicious circle of environmental degradation

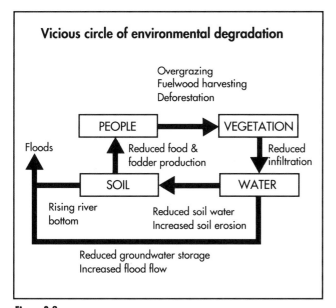

Figure 3.2

Reversal of vicious circle

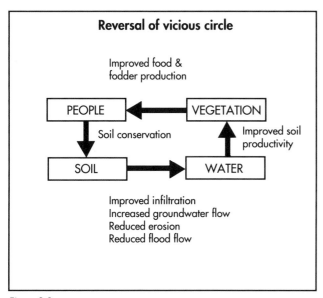

Figure 3.3

Environmental planning as a trade off process

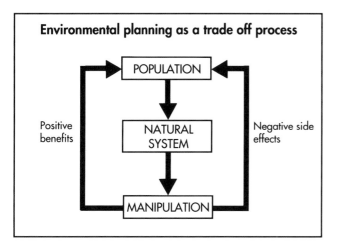

Figure 3.4

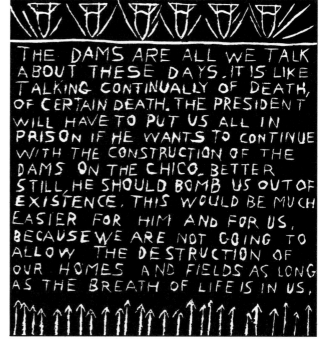

THE DAMS ARE ALL WE TALK ABOUT THESE DAYS. IT IS LIKE TALKING CONTINUALLY OF DEATH, OF CERTAIN DEATH. THE PRESIDENT WILL HAVE TO PUT US ALL IN PRISON IF HE WANTS TO CONTINUE WITH THE CONSTRUCTION OF THE DAMS ON THE CHICO. BETTER STILL, HE SHOULD BOMB US OUT OF EXISTENCE. THIS WOULD BE MUCH EASIER FOR HIM AND FOR US. BECAUSE WE ARE NOT GOING TO ALLOW THE DESTRUCTION OF OUR HOMES AND FIELDS AS LONG AS THE BREATH OF LIFE IS IN US.

Figure 3.5

Increased water competition 1980 – 2100

The freshwater available to the areas shown is limited and therefore as populations increase there is an increasing competition for water. The worst problems will be seen in Asia and Africa where the numbers of individuals to be fed on each cubic kilometre of water will increase from the present indices of 200 and 120 to 380 and 620.

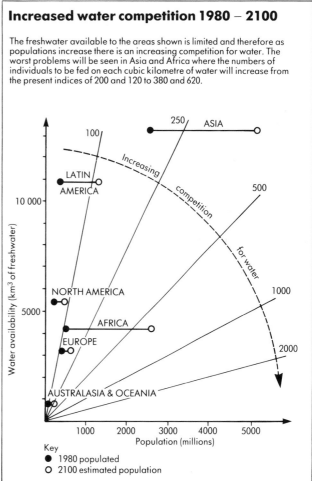

Figure 3.6

35

The Writing on the Dam

Figure 3.7

The 'technological approach' and the desire to build ever more dams has led to several ecological disasters including the billion dollar Balbina Dam in Brazil. This project destroyed 236 000 hectares of tropical forest, formed a gigantic lake of shallow stagnant water, killed millions of wild animals, flooded the local Indians' land and is continuing to cause hunger and illness to the local population - all to gain just 80 megawatts of electricity.

In Pakistan, 10 million of the 15 million hectares of land under irrigation are estimated to be affected by salinisation, waterlogging or both.

In America, the Grand Teton Dam became the world's first major dam to fail completely. Lack of proper planning in its construction led to its collapse and the destruction of 4000 homes and an estimated $2 billion worth of damage.

Such events have stimulated a worldwide reaction against the use of large dams. The era of big dam construction is now drawing to a close, partly due to peoples' protests (figure 3.7), but also due to a lack of suitable sites.

Hildyard and Goldsmith, proponents of the ecological approach put forward suggestions for assessing the feasibilty of future dam projects. They suggest any future dam project should:
* have a full assessment of the environmental effects carried out and made public
* benefit large sections of the regional population and not only the urban elite
* be labour intensive rather than capital intensive
* encourage the growing of food crops rather than cash crops for export.
* not be built if the reservoir will silt up within 100 years. (Difficult to meet in tropical conditions)
* emphasise long term resource enhancement rather than short term exploitation
* not be built for primarily political reasons.

Regardless of whether such recommendations are followed our relationship with our planet's water resource will continue to increase in complexity. This complexity is reflected in the movement towards an ecosystem approach to river basin management away from the rather simplistic engineering ot 'technological' approach of the recent past. The view of the river basin as an ecological unit (figure 3.8) allows us to bring specific problems into focus, while not losing sight of the whole.

WATER QUALITY

The most obvious area requiring an ecological perspective is water quality. The emerging water quality problems derive mainly from the application of pesticides and fertilisers which can cause contamination over very wide areas. The effects of such contamination often take many years to emerge but are no less serious because of this. Eighty per cent of disease in Developing Countries is related to poor drinking water and sanitation.

Figure 3.8

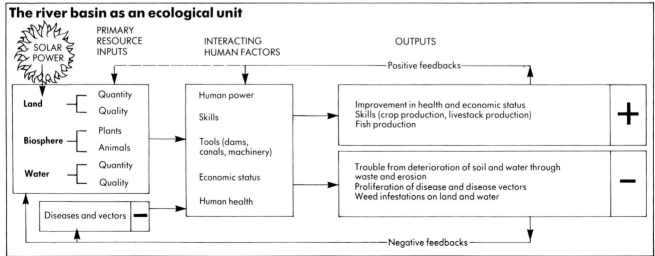

Water quantity

Water quantity, however, remains more important than quality when it comes to health in Developing Countries. A lot of water is needed to keep the body and household clean. When access to an improved water supply is obtained the improvements in health can be dramatic (figure 3.9). The upward trends in safe water supply for the rural population of the Developing Countries, although welcome (figure 3.10) are inadequate, despite the stimulus provided by the UN Drinking Water Supply and Sanitation Decade of the eighties.

A second area requiring an ecological perspective is that of shared river basins. Twelve African rivers are shared by four or more countries. In all of these basins, upstream irrigation reduces water availability for downstream countries. If management strategies are to progress to stage 4 (figure 3.11), an international code of conduct will be required, indicating how upstream countries are expected to pay adequate attention to the water interests of downstream countries. An ecosystem approach might help to lessen the risks of water, or the lack of it, becoming the source of huge social and political conflict in the 1990s.

1   What are the implications for water resource management strategies of peoples' rising expectations?
2   Do we live in a water-conscious society? Support your answer with reasons.
3   Has the engineering approach to water management been a failure or a sucess?
4   Outline the arguments for and against very large dams.
5   Why is water quantity regarded as being more important than water quality in the Developing World?
6   Why is self-reliance an important goal in the Developing World?

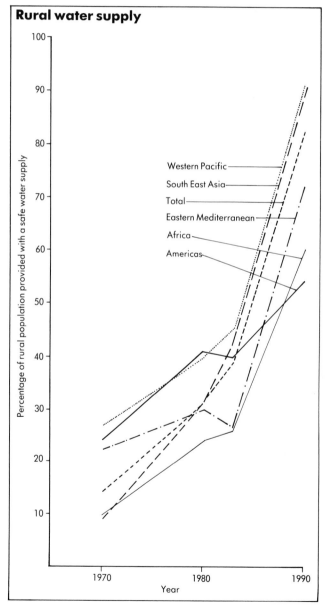

Rural water supply

Figure 3.10

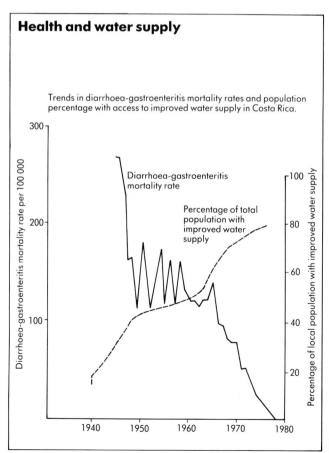

Health and water supply

Trends in diarrhoea-gastroenteritis mortality rates and population percentage with access to improved water supply in Costa Rica.

Figure 3.9

Model of stages in water resource development

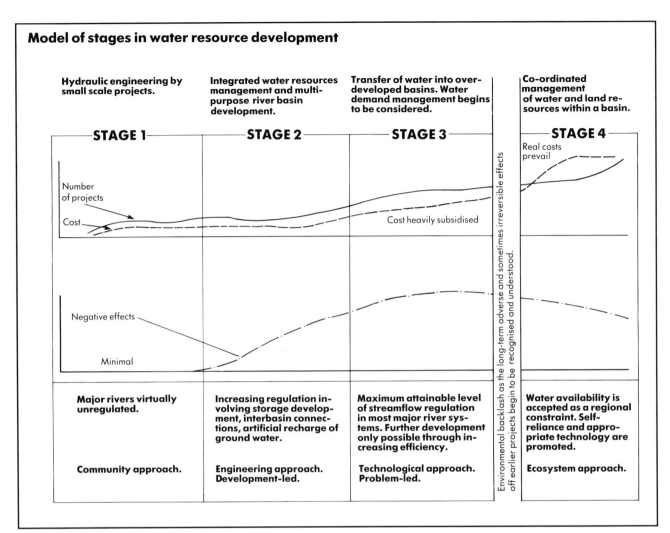

Hydraulic engineering by small scale projects.

Integrated water resources management and multi-purpose river basin development.

Transfer of water into over-developed basins. Water demand management begins to be considered.

Co-ordinated management of water and land resources within a basin.

STAGE 1 — STAGE 2 — STAGE 3 — STAGE 4

Number of projects

Cost

Real costs prevail

Cost heavily subsidised

Negative effects

Minimal

Environmental backlash as the long-term adverse and sometimes irreversible effects off earlier projects begin to be recognised and understood.

| **Major rivers virtually unregulated.** | **Increasing regulation involving storage development, interbasin connections, artificial recharge of ground water.** | **Maximum attainable level of streamflow regulation in most major river systems. Further development only possible through increasing efficiency.** | **Water availability is accepted as a regional constraint. Self-reliance and appropriate technology are promoted.** |
| **Community approach.** | **Engineering approach. Development-led.** | **Technological approach. Problem-led.** | **Ecosystem approach.** |

Figure 3.11

SUMMARY

- Ecosystems are arbitrary, natural or artificial subdivisions of the biosphere. A river basin is a prime example of an ecosystem, consisting of interacting communities of living and non living parts, within our larger planetary ecosystem, the biosphere.
- Ecosystems are made up of separate elements in which any one component cannot be modified without affecting the other component parts. It is this basic recognition of interdependence which makes the ecosystem approach so eminently suitable to problem-solving within river basin management schemes.

ASSIGNMENTS

Cadillac Desert

by Marc Reisner

Emptiness. There was nothing down there on the earth - no towns, no light, no signs of civilisation at all. Barren mountains rose duskily from the desert floor; isolated mesas and buttes broke the wind - haunted distance. I counted the minutes between clusters of lights. Six, eight, eleven, - going nine miles a minute, that was a lot of uninhabited distance in a crowded century, a lot of emptiness amid a civilisation whose success was achieved on the pretension that natural obstacles do not exist.

Then the landscape heaved upward. As suddenly as the mountains appeared, they fell away, and a vast grid iron of lights appeared out of nowhere. Salt Lake City, Orem, Draper, Provo: we were over most of the population of Utah.

More startling than its existence was the fact that it had been there only 134 years, since Brigham Young led his band of social outcasts to the old bed of a drying desert sea and proclaimed, "This is the place!". Within hours of ending their ordeal, the Mormons were digging shovels into the earth beside the streams draining the Wasatch Range, leading canals into the surrounding desert which they would convert to fields which would nourish them. Without realising it, they were laying the foundation of the most ambitious desert civilisation the world has seen. .... Fifty-six years after the first earth was turned beside City Creek, the Mormons had six million acres under full or partial irrigation in several states. In that year - 1902 - the United States government launched its own irrigation project, based on the Mormon experience, guided by Mormon laws, run largely by Mormons. The agency responsible for it, the US Bureau of Reclamation, would build the highest and largest dams in the world on rivers few believed could be controlled - the Colorado, the Sacramento, the Columbia, the Lower Snake - and run aqueducts for hundreds of miles across deserts and over mountains and through the Continental Divide in order to irrigate more millions of acres and provide water and power to a population equal to that of Italy. Thanks to irrigation, thanks to the Bureau - an agency few people know - states such as California, Arizona, and Idaho became populous and wealthy; millions settled in regions where nature, left alone, would have countenanced thousands at best; great valleys and hemispherical basins metamorphosed from desert blond to semitropic green.

... Except for the population centres of the Pacific Coast and the occasional desert metropolis - El Paso, Albuquerque, Tucson, Denver - you can drive a thousand miles in the West and encounter fewer towns than you would crossing New Hampshire. Westerners call what they have established out here a civilisation, but it would be more accurate to call it a beachhead. And if history is any guide, the odds that we can sustain it would have to be regarded as low. Only one desert civilisation, out of dozens that grew up in antiquity, has survived uninterrupted into modern times. And Egypt's approach to irrigation was fundamentally different from all the rest.

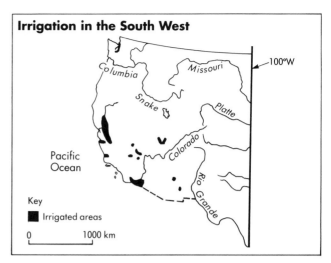

Figure 4.1

Use the information within the book to help you answer the following questions. In some cases there will not be a right or a wrong answer and you will have to back up what you say with evidence from the maps, diagrams or text.

1   The 100th meridian has been outlined on the location map. What significance does it have in terms of precipitation, temperatures and evaporation for the development of agriculture?
2   What effect has politics had on the growth and development of the various water schemes on the Colorado?
3   Technological interference is the term used to describe the work of humans in the process of river basin management. One author describes the Lower Colorado as a river which has been dismantled and rebuilt as a massive waterworks. Comment on this statement.
4   With increasing public awareness of 'Green Issues' what does the future hold for water in the west. With steadily increasing populations what are the western states doing and what could they do in the future to ensure a regular, clean, water supply to satisfy as many people as possible?
5   Describe the natural processes which are doing their best to undo the work of the water engineers in the Colorado Basin.
6   There are often problems with the division of water when it crosses a state or national boundary. Outline the problems faced and the solutions reached in this area to those questions of water division and water quality.
7   Weighing up the advantages and the disadvantages, comment on whether you think all the money has been well spent.

39

Water Quality or Water Quantity?

1 Water shortage is the major problem facing many people in the rural areas of some Third World countries. Describe the effects this might have and outline how well these problems have been dealt with by the large multi-purpose schemes.

2 Describe the different pollution problems facing Developed and Developing World water authorities and outline the possible solutions to these problems.

3 Outline the 'quality and quantity' problems faced by any river management scheme you have studied and describe the merits of the alternative solutions.

4 'The larger the scheme the greater the problems.' Discuss this concept in relation to any named river management scheme.

Figure 4.2   Source: New Internationalist

From Flood Irrigation to Perennial Irrigation on the Lower Nile

MAIN STAGES OF NILE IRRIGATION DEVELOPMENT

Stage 1 The first aricultural revolution in the Nile valley arrived with the start of artifical irrigation, including deliberate flooding and draining by sluice gates. Such basin irrigation schemes were established by the First Dynasty 3050 BC. Although this limited control of the flood waters was an improvement on total dependence on the vagaries of the annual Nile flood, the variations in flood level remained critical, and crops could only be grown after the flood had receded.

Stage 2 The second agricultural revolution came with the introduction of lift irrigation. The first mechanised water lift was the shaduf, introduced circa 1550 - 1307 BC (see figure 4.3). This was followed by the more efficient Persian wheel or sakia circa 323 - 330 BC. These lifting devices permitted increased realiability in years of low flood and the introduction of limited summer crops. This system or irrigation continued largely unchanged until the middle of the 19th century. In fact the shaduf, sakia and archimedes screw are still in regular use in rural Egypt today.

Stage 3 The impetus for the third agricultural revolution was provided by an Albanian soldier of fortune, Mohammed Ali Pasha, who rose to become ruler of Egypt in 1805. In an effort to maximise his revenues, Mohammed Ali introduced cash crops such as sugar cane, vegetables, fruit and in particular, cotton. The production of cotton necessitated a radical change in the irrigation system, since it required regular watering and needed to be protected from inundation during the flood. Controlled year round or perennial irrigation was required but the natural variations in water levels remained an obstacle to development in the delta area. This problem acted as a catalyst for the first artifical structures across the Nile - the Delta Barrages (1843-1861). Fortunately Mohammed Ali was dissuaded by his engineers from using the stone from the pyramids in the construction!

The major landmark in irrigation development in Sudan was the completion of the Senner Dam on the Blue Nile, which now irrigates an area of over 2 million feddans (a feddan equals 0.42 hectares) in the Gezira.

Discussion here is limited to water use in Sudan and Egypt as these countries have been by far the major users of Nile water and use by other countries may be regarded as negligible. The growth of Egyptian and Sudanese populations and cultivated and cropped areas is shown in tables 4a and 4b. The disparity in agricultural development revealed in the tables has been increased with the completion of the Aswan High Dam in 1964, which has so far brought immense benefits from increased irrigated areas, increased yields and increased cropping intensities and above all cushioning Egypt from the worse effects of the recurring Sahelian drought.

One of the main objectives of constructing the High Aswan Dam was the conversion of the traditional basin irrigation system, with its one crop a year, to a perennial system producing two or three crops per year. The aim is to double the yield of this area and the resulting changes are illustrated in figures 4.5 and 4.6, forming perhaps a fourth agricultural revolution.

GROWTH OF POPULATION AND CROPPED AREAS IN EGYPT

Year	Estimated population (million)	Cultivable area ('000 feddans)	Cropped area ('000 feddans)	Cropping intensity (%)
1821	2.51 to 4.23	3053	3053	100
1846	4.50 to 5.29	3746	3746	100
1882	7.93	4758	5754	121
1897	9.72	4943	6725	136
1907	11.19	5374	7595	141
1917	12.72	5309	7729	146
1927	14.18	5544	8522	154
1937	15.92	5312	8302	156
1947	18.97	5761	9133	159
1960	26.09	5900	10200	173
1966	30.08	6000	10400	173
1970	33.20	5900	10900	185
1975	37.00	5700	10700	188
1986	49.70	6000	11400	190

Table 4a

GROWTH OF POPULATION AND CROPPED AREAS IN SUDAN

Year	Estimated population (million)	Cultivable area ('000 feddans)	Cropped area ('000 feddans)	Cropping intensity (%)
1905	3.0	100	?	?
1930	5.0	400	?	?
1940	6.0	1100	?	?
1957	10.3	2245	1216	54
1970	14.3	3218	2348	73
1980	19.2	4385	3600	82
1986	22.6	4155	2772	67

Table 4b

Read the summary of Nile irrigation development and study the photos and diagrams below.

1 The landscape of the Zinnar basin around the village of Musha is undergoing rapid change after almost 3000 years of remaining unchanged. Describe the advantages of the change over from basin irrigation to perennial irrigation to the farmers in Musha. How will the landscape change further over the next 30 years?

2 Convert the statistics in tables 4a and 4b into graphs. Compare and contrast the development of irrigation in Egypt and Sudan. Explain the disparity between the rates of development.

3 Explain why the shaduf, sakia and archimedes screw remain commonplace in rural Egypt today.

4 Until recently the availability of Nile water had gradually increased, keeping pace with the increase in population. However, Egypt and Sudan are now faced with the prospect of continuing increasing population but with only limited further water available for agricultural expansion. Outline possible ways in which this problem might be averted.

Figure 4.3 Shaduf, Niger

Figure 4.4 Water pumping station on the Nile

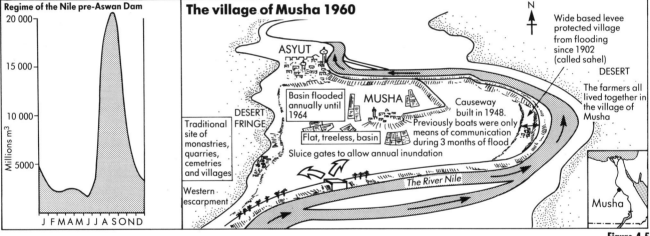

Regime of the Nile pre-Aswan Dam

Millions m³ (axis: 5000, 10 000, 15 000, 20 000)
J F M A M J J A S O N D

The village of Musha 1960

ASYUT

MUSHA

Wide based levee protected village from flooding since 1902 (called sahel)

DESERT

The farmers all lived together in the village of Musha

Basin flooded annually until 1964

Causeway built in 1948. Previously boats were only means of communication during 3 months of flood

Flat, treeless basin

Sluice gates to allow annual inundation

Traditional site of monastries, quarries, cemeteries and villages

DESERT FRINGE

Western escarpment

The River Nile

Musha

Figure 4.5

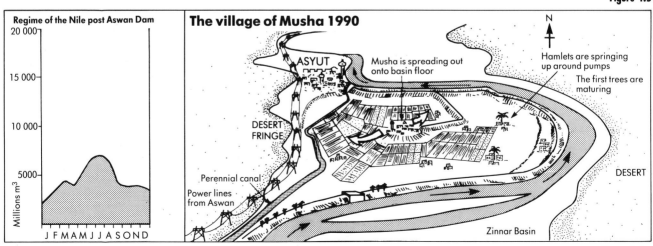

Regime of the Nile post Aswan Dam

Millions m³ (axis: 5000, 10 000, 15 000, 20 000)
J F M A M J J A S O N D

The village of Musha 1990

ASYUT

Musha is spreading out onto basin floor

Hamlets are springing up around pumps

The first trees are maturing

DESERT FRINGE

Perennial canal

Power lines from Aswan

DESERT

Zinnar Basin

Figure 4.6

The Aswan Dam - anatomy of a megasystem

1 What evidence is there from figure 4.9 that the closing of the sluice gates of the Aswan High Dam in 1964 and the subsequent completion of the project in 1971 have resulted in control of the River Nile's regime?

2 Create a balance sheet for the Aswan project with a summary of benefits to Egypt on one side and the costs (environmental, social and economic) on the other.

3a Advertisements on Egyptian televison encourage viewers to turn off taps and guard against waste. What other conservation measures might the Egyptians adopt to save water?

b With reference to figures 4.7 and 4.10 explain why such conservation measures are likely to become increasingly important.

ESTIMATED PRESENT WATER USE IN EGYPT

Volume in billion cubic metres

Inflow

Aswan release	55.5

Outflow

Drainage to sea and seepage	17.5

Water use

Municipal and industrial	2.4
Evapotranspiration (irrigation)	33.6
Evaporation from water surfaces	2.0

Table 4c

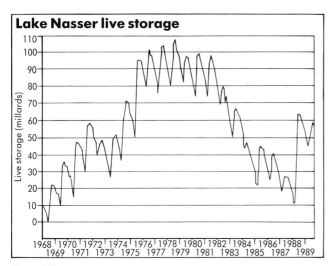

Figure 4.7

Figure 4.8 Aswan Dam and power station

ASWAN DAM : KEY FACTS

Benefits

• The control of high floods and the supplementing of low floods. Egypt has therefore saved the monetary costs of covering damage from high and low floods since 1964.

• The increase in cultivated land area through reclamation and the increase of crop production of the existing land through the conversion from basin to perennial irrigation.

• Navigation on the Nile has improved and is now possible all the year round rather than being seasonal. This has given a particular boost to the tourist industry.

• Electricity generation by the dam now supplies one-quarter of Egypt's total requirements. In 1976, Egypt completed an impressive rural electrification programme that was only feasible because of the Aswan's HEP output.

• Lake Nasser's resources are potentially economic, including land cultivation and settlement, fishing and tourism.

These benefits to Egypt are generally undisputed. It is the relative significance of the following side effects which have generated debate and controversy.

Negative side effects

• Water loss through seepage and evaporation is likely to affect the water supply needed for development plans. Although the water loss measured so far lies within or close to the engineer's predictions, the accompanying rise in water tables does not.

• At one time the Nile deposited 120 million tonnes of sediment at its delta each year. As this fertile silt is now trapped by Lake Nasser, the farmers of the delta have had to turn to costly artifical fertilisers. The lack of silt has also led to coastal erosion of the northern delta and the complete collapse of the sardine fishing industry. Although the new fisheries catch on Lake Nasser outweighs the loss of the Mediterranean sardine fishery, overall this economic gain should not be allowed to obscure the socio-economic problems imposed on the sardine fishing people and their families. The silt free, clear water of the Nile below Aswan is also causing riverbed degradation. Another problem caused by the lack of silt relates to the brickmaking industry. Silt is the basic component of Egyptian bricks and production dropped by one-third between 1970 and 1980. This may prove to be another case for industrial relocation.

• Soil salinity is increasing and land is becoming waterlogged due to seepage from the river and canal beds and the lack of efficient drainage schemes in areas of perennial irrigation. The previously 15 metre underground water table has been raised to only 3 metres on average. The adverse effects on land productivity, houses and construction projects are difficult to quantify.

• The transfer of the Egyptian and Sudanese Nubians from their 'drowned' valley settlements to new sites may be regarded as either a drastic social cost of the development or a social-economic gain for the relocatees - 100 000 people in all were relocated and although they enjoy a better educational system, improved health care and communications, the majority of older Nubians still harbour resentment over their enforced move and speak wistfully of their previous lands.

• Increased contact with water through irrigation extension schemes, and in particular the conversion from basin to perennial irrigation, is associated with an increase in water based diseases such as schistosmiasis (bilharzia). Again conflicting evidence exists as to the prevalence of this endemic disease in Egypt. Some areas have recorded a drop in its incidence due to improved water supplies and better sanitation facilities. Other areas have recorded a change in schistosomiasis to a more severe form which previous to the control system at Aswan was non-existent.

• The water hyacinth, *Eichornia crasspipes*, has invaded the newly formed aquatic system of Lake Nasser. Such weeds increase the rate of transpiration dramatically. Once established, water weeds are difficult, if not impossible, to eradicate. The Egyptians have dosed their canals and irrigation drains with massive quantities of herbicides, at unknown ecological cost, in the battle to get rid of the water hyacinth. However, this spraying operation is recognised to be no more than a holding operation.

• The great weight of the water and its related dam is believed to be responsible for increased seismic activity in the Aswan area.

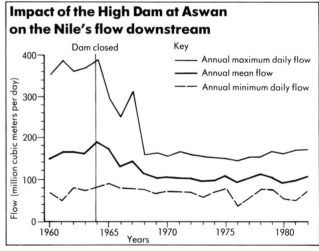

Figure 4.9

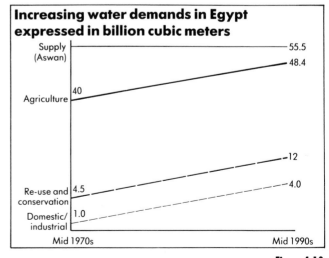

Figure 4.10

Water Statistics - the Nile

1 From table 4d choose two years with contrasting annual discharges. Draw annotated diagrams to show the major differences and describe the effects each might have on the farmers further down river.

2 Calculate the mean monthly average. Which months show the greatest percentage variability?

3 You have been asked to make up a report proving the effectiveness of the High Dam at Aswan in preventing floods. Illustrate your report with any relevant diagrams, statistics or charts.

	MEASURED FLOWS IN MILLIONS M³												
Year	Jan	Feb	March	April	May	June	July	Aug	Sep	Oct	Nov	Dec	Total
1912	3380	2470	1890	1410	1180	984	3170	18500	18200	11100	5690	4170	72140
1913	3260	2040	1480	1280	1170	1470	1740	6500	12200	7540	4120	2830	45630
1914	1720	1150	1070	947	998	975	2010	19400	20000	16500	10700	6930	82480
1915	4510	3090	2130	1360	1170	1460	2850	10700	14900	14700	8090	5270	70230
1916	3850	2400	1610	1180	1090	1340	5010	25000	26600	22400	13300	7880	111660
1917	5370	3910	3580	2320	1680	1860	4830	17500	27800	22800	11600	7460	110710
1918	5270	3990	4330	4090	3960	3230	5190	13600	17700	11100	6210	4580	83250
1919	3440	2180	1910	1520	1350	1520	3680	16600	20800	12600	6140	4410	76350
1920	3320	2090	1600	1370	1220	1710	5370	18200	17800	15000	8960	5570	82410
1921	3820	2370	1760	1330	1180	1300	2980	15400	19600	14800	7590	4700	76830
1922	3530	2090	1460	996	801	900	3280	18800	23600	15900	8240	4880	84480
1923	3030	2350	1540	1200	1380	2050	4440	20100	21400	16200	7250	5170	86110
1924	4000	2650	1850	1320	1470	1630	5050	18000	22300	14300	7990	5590	86150
1925	3840	2540	1830	1370	1260	1580	3910	13400	16600	12500	6450	4480	69760
1926	3440	2150	1640	1340	1330	2390	4360	19200	20600	14500	8330	5230	84510
1927	3940	2910	2030	1440	1300	1290	4180	15600	18300	13300	6090	4010	74390
1928	2600	1630	1310	1160	1320	2560	6290	18200	20000	12400	7300	4820	79590
1929	3670	2400	1770	1340	1390	3250	8770	23200	24500	18000	9910	5580	103780
1930	4250	2950	2120	1540	1530	1660	4400	18300	17600	11800	5640	4020	75810
1931	2350	1790	1500	1220	1090	1140	2850	15900	21300	15000	8620	4840	77600
1932	3580	2260	1680	1320	1270	1700	4280	18900	22900	13800	7720	5050	84460
1933	4170	3470	2850	1680	1600	1800	3280	13100	22100	15300	9150	5940	84440
1934	4340	2960	2110	1550	1440	1700	6050	20500	23700	16400	8370	5250	94370
1935	4170	2990	2170	1530	1520	2330	7100	21300	24100	17700	8220	5200	98330
1936	4000	2800	2180	1560	1450	1530	5490	19000	23900	15800	7420	4550	89680
1937	3340	2100	1740	1360	1130	1500	3950	19800	22300	14300	6050	4590	82160
1938	3540	2160	2160	1560	1280	1450	3710	23200	27800	19500	9520	5520	101400
1939	4120	3240	2430	1960	2220	1960	3920	13100	18400	13000	7980	4770	77100
1940	3420	2130	2430	1810	1310	1330	3050	15300	18000	10900	4630	3370	67080
1941	2260	1830	2070	1630	1100	1550	4320	12000	14400	11100	8040	4540	64840
1942	3200	2330	2460	2310	1930	1710	4530	20300	20300	14900	6360	4240	84570
1943	3230	1910	2570	2080	1670	1480	2670	15600	24700	14200	6840	4270	81220
1944	3070	2000	2660	2270	1890	1810	4180	16700	18100	12600	5240	3850	74370
1945	2590	1340	2550	2150	1580	1610	3580	14900	18900	16400	8410	5360	79370
1946	3840	2550	2360	2310	2120	1340	6130	25100	27800	15800	9100	5980	104430
1947	4420	3480	3180	2520	2770	2850	3170	14900	22500	15000	6550	4640	85980
1948	3710	2950	2510	2370	2330	1530	5430	16600	19300	15700	9790	5190	87410
1949	3610	2830	2440	2400	2510	1900	4080	18100	20400	14300	7490	4840	84900
1950	3860	2900	2500	2390	2530	2280	4610	20800	22500	14800	6610	4460	90240
1951	3390	2240	2270	2340	2150	1180	2850	15400	17800	12000	7790	4940	74250
1952	3280	2380	2680	2100	1610	1690	3210	14900	21100	12500	6240	3710	75400
1953	2790	1890	2180	2410	1600	1460	3860	22000	20800	13900	6330	4120	83340
1954	2870	1830	2550	2270	1820	1180	5630	24800	28300	20500	8550	5050	105350
1955	3820	2710	2080	2280	2490	2180	4320	19200	22700	18000	7410	4580	91770
1956	3580	2800	2350	2310	2250	2370	5780	19700	20700	18400	12400	5760	98700
1957	3990	3110	2380	2630	3010	2960	4450	17600	21400	9920	4890	3380	79720
1958	2560	1850	2080	2150	1700	1300	5000	24600	24500	15700	8410	4870	94720
1959	3430	2420	2250	2420	2340	1620	3370	18700	29600	16600	9670	5090	97510
1960	3650	2420	2220	2460	2370	1730	3790	17100	20900	14500	6610	3740	81490
1961	2940	1980	2210	2540	2220	1310	5400	26600	27000	18600	9410	5680	101890
1962	4140	3080	2780	2900	2840	3140	4690	15800	22500	26700	7260	4730	90560
1963	3710	2960	2700	2550	2880	3310	5310	20400	21800	13200	6150	5110	90080
1964	4770	3570	3040	2550	3480	3840	5840	24900	27000	18300	12300	6980	116570
1965	5880	5250	4940	3660	3660	4540	5600	13400	17300	12400	9770	5750	92150
1966	4380	3140	2510	2580	3570	2330	5480	12300	16900	11400	5020	4870	74480
1967	2745	3390	3888	3557	4480	5869	6618	8921	7096	12610	5598	4670	69540
1968	3281	4228	4063	3700	4785	6350	6065	6105	4180	3795	3590	3240	53800
1969	2900	3700	3970	3660	4870	6570	6710	6890	4200	3810	3640	3390	53510
1970	3060	3980	4090	3920	5420	6520	6720	6110	4285	3750	3395	3245	54700
1971	3554	3785	4275	3940	5475	6490	6965	625	4445	3775	3670	3295	55890
1972	3450	4020	4240	4040	5290	6535	6990	6290	4245	3745	3590	3025	55470
1973	2610	3505	4380	4000	5360	6580	7005	6380	4235	3855	3920	3580	55430

Table 4d   Monthly and annual discharge statistics for the Nile 1912-1973. Source: Hydrology of the River Nile, Mamdouh Shahin, 1985.

The Rhône

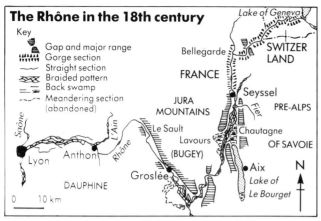

Figure 4.11

The upper section of the Rhône between Lake Geneva and Seyssel follows a glacial trough as it winds through the Jura. Between Seyssel and Le Sault it follows the path of glacially overdeepened troughs carved out along synclines of weak sedimentary rock. These were subsequently filled with sand and gravel by deposition from melting ice. This plain section suffered from braiding and shifting channels with large swamps developing in the wider sections. Every summer the people of the Rhône valley suffered from the devastating floods brought on by the river. From Le Sault the braiding still existed but added to this there were a series of rapids as the river crossed some limestone. The river enters the Mediterranean after depositing its remaining sediment load in the channels of the Rhône delta.

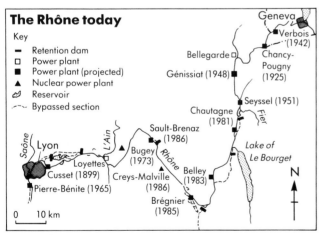

Figure 4.12

In the nineteenth century life in the upper valley was closely linked to the rhythm of the river. Floods bringing flows ten times the average forced the villagers to settle on the terraces up above the level of the floodplain. Small embankments and flood control measures stood little chance of controlling

the incredible power of the river. Navigation was limited to small flat-bottomed boats but there were problems with rock bars, gravel bars and the floods themselves. River control started in earnest in the period after World War II with the completion of the dam at Génissiat which led to the drowning of the gorges of the upper valley. The river was canalised and bypass channels were built away from the worst braided sections. The new security of the fertile floodplains attracted farmers and a lot of land was reclaimed and used to grow maize and market vegetables. The bypassed areas of marsh land and braided sections were turned into nature reserves. In the 1970s the emphasis turned to the lower Rhône with a whole series of HEP stations and dams with the power being used to stimulate industrial development as part of a decentralisation regional policy. The power was also used to carry water to areas to the west of the delta where water shortages had restricted farm development.

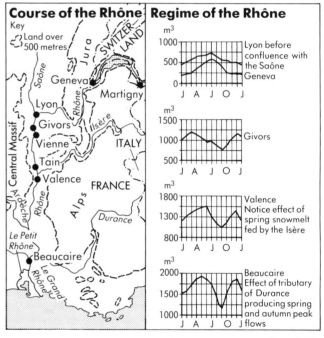

Figure 4.13

1 Describe the main features of a 'multi purpose scheme' of river basin management.
2 Describe the regime of the River Rhône at Geneva and Valence and try to explain the differences.
3 In what way can river control be a spur to the industrial and agricultural development of an area like the Rhône.
4 Describe the features of the climate of the lower Rhône and the delta area which make irrigation agriculture necessary.
5 From information you have researched draw an annotated map of the Rhône valley showing the main features of river control.

46

Glossary

Aquifer - A layer of rock which can absorb and hold a great deal of water.

Bankfull Discharge - The volume of water within a section of a river when the river channel is full to the top of its bank.

Carrying Capacity - Any ecosystem can support a limited number of people on a self-reliant basis. In water management terms, the finite amount of water available within a drainage basin can be measured and used to calculate the capacity of the basin for development and, by inference, the maximum population the basin could support.

Corrasion - The process of erosion of the river bed and banks by the load being carried by the river. The resulting effect is called **abrasion**.

Corrosion - The erosion of the river bed and banks by the process of solution.

Drainage Basin - The land which is drained by a network of streams.

Drip Irrigation - The controlled addition water to the land via a pipe either on the surface or below ground.

Ecosystem - A large scale or small scale collection of interacting communities within a specific environment. Ecosystems are a useful way of examining relationships and interdependencies.

Ecosystem Approach - An approach which argues that negative side effects should be quantified at as early in the planning stage as possible and balanced against the intended benefits. An ecological audit should ensure that any proposed development is both appropriate and sustainable. Such audits have spared rivers as diverse as the Narmada in India and the Loire in France from unnecessary development.

Flood Irrigation - The diverting of flood water on to prepared farmland. This is a traditional opportunistic farming activity which usually involves some method of water retention, e.g. low walls or embankments.

Floodplains - The floor of a river valley, adjacent to the river channel, over which a river flows in times of flood. As a river recedes the river deposits a fertile silt known as **alluvium**. A **scroll** is a low, curving ridge running parallel with the loop of a **meander** or river bend. **Ox-bow lakes** are often found on floodplains. These crescent-shaped lakes are former meander curves which have been cut-off from the river channel when it changed course. A **levee** is a raised bank flanking the river channel and standing above the the level of the floodplain. It is formed naturally by the river in times of flood, but is often subsequently reinforced as a defense against flooding in river management schemes.

Groundwater Mining - The extraction of water which occupies pores, cracks and other spaces in crystal rocks. Groundwater includes rainwater which has percolated through the soil and into the rock (meteoric water) as well as water which has been retained in sedimentary rocks since their formation (fossilwater) and water which has risen from deep igneous sources (juvenile water). The term groundwater mining implies abstraction at a faster rate than the groundwater is being replaced.

Hydraulic Action - The force exerted by running water on the river bed banks without the use of the material the river is carrying (load).

Hydrosphere - The water on the surface of the earth: the water component of the global system.

Infiltration Capacity - The maximum rate at which water can penetrate the soil. If the infiltration capacity of the soil is exceeded overland flow or runoff occurs.

Regime - The regime of a river is the rhythm of its seasonal flow of water.

Saturation - The condition in which the pores, cracks and joints of a permeable rock are filled with water. The rock then temporarily becomes impermeable.

Technological Approach - The technological approach to river basin management sees the regulation of any river as a series of engineering problems. These problems of storage, diversion, extraction, irrigation, navigation, salinisation and purification can all be solved at a price. Unfortunately the planned cost has rarely in the past included the additional costs arising from the inevitable side effects - draining of valleys, habitat disruption, siltation of reservoirs, loss of alluvium, seepage, erosion of the river bed, land degradation and displacement of local populations.

Selected bibliography

Chapter 1

Textbooks

Human Activity and Environmental Processes, KJ Gregory and DE Walling, John Wiley, 1987.

Physical Environment and Human Activities, J Porter, Oxford University Press, 1989.

Taming the Flood, J Purseglove, Oxford University Press, 1988.

Physical Geography: A Systems Approach, RJ Chorley and BA Kennedy, Prentice Hall, 1971.

The Social and Environmental Effects of Large Dams, E Goldsmith and N Hildyard, Wadebridge Ecological Centre, 1984.

The Human Impact, A Goudie, Basil Blackwell, 1981.

Spaceship Earth, N Calder, Channel 4, Viking, 1991.

The Environment, V Bishop and R Prosser, Collins, 1990.

World Resources 1986, World Resources Institute, Basic Books, 1988.

World Resources 1987, World Resources Institute, Basic Books, 1989.

World Resources 1988-89, World Resources Institute, Basic Books, 1990.

Journals and magazines

Water: Thirsty for Life: The Power of Water, The New Internationalist, No. 207, May 1990.

Mighty Torrents and Mankind, G Petts, Geographical Magazine, September 1987.

Water: the Essential Essence, Geographical Magazine, May 1977.

India's Unwanted Dam, F Pearce, New Scientist, No. 1753, January 1991.
Africa in the 1990s, The New Internationalist, No. 208, June 1990.
Giants that are Stalking the Earth, F Pearce, Environment Guardian, June 22, 1990.
Video
Series *'The Savage Strikes Back' Follow the rainbow; local campaign against the Narmada Dam in Bihar, India*, Channel 4, 1991.

Chapter 2
Textbooks
Social and Environmental Effects of Large Dams, E Goldsmith and N Hildyard, Wadebridge Ecological Centre, 1984.
Case Studies: Large Dams, E Goldsmith and N Hildyard, Wadebridge Ecological Centre, 1984.
Cadillac Desert, M Reisner, Penguin, 1989.
A River No More, P Fradkin, University of Arizona Press, 1981.
Troubled Waters, MT El Ashry, World Resources Institute, 1986.
Strategies for River Basin Management, Ed M Falkenmark, D Reidel, 1985.
Journals
The People Who Live in a Desert, The Economist, 11 May 1986.
Phoenix Drowning in Arizona Desert, New Scientist, 27 May 1983.
Showdown at Noon, The Guardian, 27 March, 1985.
Water for the West, The Economist, Volume 310, 1988.
Sun-dried West, The Economist, Volume 307, 11 June 1988.
Running on Empty, Weekend Guardian, 6 January, 1990.
This Little Water Went to Market, The Economist, 3 April 1986.
Rivers, Do They Know They're Systems? Geography Review, Volume 1, No. 1, August 1983.
Landforms in the Grand Canyon, Geography Review, Volume 2, No. 2, October 1984.
Do Water Markets Work? Water Resources Research, Volume 23, No. 7, June 1983.
Water Wars, Geographical Magazine, May 1991.
Videos
Series on the politics of water *'Water Wars'*, The American West, BBC 2, May 1991.
'Colorado 1 and 2', schools geography programme, BBC, 1992.
'Vanishing Earth' - soils; sections on Burkina Faso and the American West (Phoenix and San Joaquin Valley, BBC, 1986.

Chapter 3
Textbooks
Water Resources: Issues and Strategies, AT McDonald and D Kay, Longman, 1988.

Strategies for River Basin Management, M Falkenmark, U Lohm (Ed), D Reidel, 1987.
The Biosphere, G Evelyn Hutchinson et al, Scientific America, 1970.
River Basin Planning: Theory and Practice, Suranjit K Saha and CJ Barrow, John Wiley, 1982.
Journals and magazines
New Ecological Approach to the Water Cycle, M Falkenmark, Ambio, Volume 13, No. 3, 1984.
Water-Related Limitations to Local Development, M Falkenmark, et al, Ambio, Volume 16, No. 4, 1987.
Water Management Strategies Needed for the 21st Century, M Falkenmark, Water International, Volume 12, No. 3, 1987.
Hydropolitics, Geographical Magazine, February - April, 1991.

Chapter 4
Textbooks
The Nile: Resource Evaluation, Resource Management, Hydropolitics and Legal Issues, PP Howell, School of Oriental and African Studies, 1990.
Agrarian Transformation in Egypt, NS Hopkins, Westview Press, 1987.
Agrarian Change in Egypt, S Radwan and E Lee, Croom Helm, 1987.
Cadillac Desert, M Reisner, Penguin, 1989.
Population and Development in Rural Egypt, A Kelley, Duke Press, 1982.
Dams, People and Development: The Aswan High Dam, HM Fahim, Pergamon Press, 1981.
Hydrology of the Nile Basin, M Shahin, Elsevier, 1985.
Journals and periodicals
Riches of the Nile, G Petts, Geographical Magazine, March 1988.
The Rising Nile Has No Mercy, G King, African Business, September 1988.
Mixed Blessings of the Flooding in Sudan, M Wright, New Scientist, September 1988.
State of the Nile Environment, E Essam El-Hinnawi, Water Supply and Management, Volume 4, 1980.
The Nile, A Silverish Lining to Sudan's Clouds, The Economist, August 1988.
Nile Water Management and the Aswan High Dam, Water Resources Development, Volume 5, No. 1, March 1989.
Nile in Trouble: 4000 Years On, G Power, World Water, August 1988.
The Rhône, Geographical Magazine, November 1987.